Glass Candlesticks

of the

DEPRESSION ERA

VOLUME 2

IDENTIFICATION AND VALUE GUIDE

Gene & Cathy

Florence

cb

COLLECTOR BOOKS

A Division of Schroeder Publishing Co., Inc.

FRONT COVER:

Top left: Indiana #301 Garland, $35.00. **Top right:** New Martinsville Moondrops "wings," $40.00. **Middle:** Indiana Willow/Orleandor, $45.00. **Bottom left:** A. H. Heisey Mars #113, $35.00. **Bottom right:** Fostoria #2484, $75.00.

BACK COVER:

Top left: Fostoria #2639 Duo, $75.00. **Top right:** Paden City Crow's Foot Round #890, Oriental Garden Etch, $40.00. **Middle:** Cambridge Rosalie Etch #703, $35.00. **Bottom left:** A. H. Heisey Crystolite #1503 2-lite, $50.00. **Bottom right:** Dolphin Reproduction of Boston Sandwich, $20.00.

Cover design: Beth Summers
Book design: Lisa Henderson
Cover photography: Charles R. Lynch

COLLECTOR BOOKS
P.O. Box 3009
Paducah, Kentucky 42002–3009

www.collectorbooks.com

The current values in this book should be used only as a guide. They are not intended to set prices, which vary from one section of the country to another. Auction prices, as well as dealer prices, vary greatly and are affected by condition as well as demand. Neither the authors nor the publisher assumes responsibility for any losses that might be incurred as a result of consulting this guide.

Searching for a Publisher?

We are always looking for people knowledgeable within their fields. If you feel that there is a real need for a book on your collectible subject and have a large comprehensive collection, contact Collector Books.

Proudly printed and bound in the
United States of America

Contents

Preface 4

How to Use This Book .4

Acknowledgments .5

Amber 6

Amethyst 15

Black 24

Blue 37

Crystal 62

Green 136

Multicolor 159

Pink 161

Purple 181

Red 183

Smoke 195

White 196

Yellow 205

Index 218

Bibliography 221

Preface

After writing the first candlestick book, we started accumulating additional candles for a second book. It had been over twenty years since a candlestick book had been published and we mentioned in the first book that it was barely a beginning in the vast world of American glass candlesticks. Little did we know that a book on candles would open the floodgates for other books. At last count, we knew of eleven others. We slowed down and worked on other ideas including two more Pattern Identification books and another on Hazel-Atlas even though we had already photographed enough for half another book. We decided, in order to do a second book, we would have to illustrate, in color, as many candles as we could that were not pictured in those other books. We believe this second book pictures over 100 candles never previously pictured.

This book covers all forms of candles, from candlesticks to candelabra. Terminology used is always that of the company catalogs, if possible, and not necessarily the terms that the present world acknowledges. We were taught the Latin ending *brum* was singular and *bra* was plural. This was not necessarily true in older glass company catalogs. We do know the difference, even though it is not specified in the text at times.

Hopefully, you will enjoy our efforts. The saturation of candlestick books should make this our last book on this subject matter.

How to Use This Book

This book is arranged by color, similar to the format of our stemware book. A few minor differences are incorporated; for instance, all crystal is in one section whether decorated, satinized, cut, or etched. Within the color sections, candles are arranged by company and pattern. There are a few liberties taken within an individual company section in order to fit the category and layout for the book; but, all in all, this seems to be the easiest way for new (as well as seasoned) collectors to find an unknown candle for which they are searching. For example, if you have a blue candle (any shade of blue) look in that color section first. If not there, try the crystal section next. There are more crystal candles pictured than any other types since there are more of those found.

If the candle has a name (true or nickname), we have generally used that first, rather than the assigned company catalog number, though the catalog number (for both the candle blank and etching) is listed where known. You may also note that like-numbered candle lines may have varying prices due to certain etches and/or colors being more desirable to collectors. **All prices are for one candle and not a pair. Realize that colored candles are generally worth more than crystal, and that these prices are only a guide.** Blue or red candles are generally more highly prized than amber, pink, or green. There are too many variables to price every color within the guidelines of this book. We asked for several dealers' opinions in pricing the candles, but the final responsibility lies entirely with us.

One final note regarding size notations; all measurements are for height, unless otherwise specified. When two measurements are given, the first is for height, the second for length/width.

We hope you find this volume a welcome addition to your reference library on glassware.

Acknowledgments

We have greatly benefited from the efforts of many people who helped us assemble glass and information for our books. This volume was no exception. My wife, Cathy, routinely aids the process of identifying and researching glassware. She spent many hours examining line numbers and obscure pattern names for candlesticks while I was working on other projects. About the time we were to finish work on this book, she suddenly had a stroke which caused this to be very late to the publishers. Our lives changed in an instant and books were the last thing on our minds. At this writing, I'm happy to report she is mending nicely.

Most of the photographs in this book were taken by Charles R. Lynch, official photographer for Collector Books. He generally likes to take individual pictures, and gets anxious when he sees all the dangling prisms on some of the larger candlesticks. (It takes a while for all of them to stabilize every time the candle is moved in a different way). It literally took us years to get all these photos accumulated. Mike Neilson supplied shots of candlesticks from the Cambridge Glass Museum and from Lynn Welker's collection.

Too many dealers have sold us candlesticks and furnished pricing information to acknowledge all of them here; but we would particularly like to express our gratitude to Dick and Pat Spencer who repeatedly brought candles to Paducah to be photographed always asking if we needed any others. Usually, we expect Heisey candles from Dick and Pat, but they surprised us with a variety from other companies. Also, Dan Tucker found some exceptional examples and sent digitals of them for our use. John and Evelyn Knowles, Norman Woodson, and Ron and Barbara Mavks lent candles from their collections.

The staff at Collector Books has worked tirelessly in and around our life upheavals. Beth Summers did the cover design; Lisa Henderson accomplished the layout. There were many shapes and sizes to deal with by the staff, as you can see by the variety of candles shown.

As with the stemware book, there were vast quantities of individual transparencies to sort and arrange. All additional quandaries were given to Collector Books editor, Gail Ashburn. We are very grateful for everyone's assistance and sincerely hope you benefit from all our endeavors.

AMBER

Company: **Bryce Brothers Co.**
Pattern: **Aquarius**
Color: Amber
Size: 4½"
Value: $15.00

Company: **Cambridge Glass Co.**
Pattern: **Gadroon #3500/32**
Color: Amber
Size: 6½"
Value: $100.00

Company: **Cambridge Glass Co.**
Pattern: **Square #3797/67**
Color: Amber
Size: 4½" wide
Value: $50.00

Company: **Central Glass Works**
Pattern: **Spiral #1426**
Color: Amber
Size: 4"
Value: $15.00

Company: **Central Glass Works**
Pattern: **Unidentified**
Color: Amber
Size: 2¾"
Value: $22.50

Company: **Duncan and Miller Glass Co.**
Pattern: **Quilted Diamond #44**
Color: Amber
Size: 3¾"
Value: $25.00

Company: **Duncan and Miller Glass Co.**
Pattern: **Ripple #101**
Color: Amber
Size: 3"
Value: $15.00

Company: Fenton Art Glass Co.
Pattern: Silvertone #1011,
            3-toe, club shape
Color: Amber
Size: 1¾"
Value: $12.00

Company: Fostoria Glass Co.
Pattern: Lily #2352
Color: Amber
Size: 6"
Value: $35.00

AMBER

Company: Fostoria Glass Co.
Pattern: Fairfax #2375, Acanthus
       etch #282
Color: Amber
Size: 3"
Value: $35.00

AMBER

Company: H.C. Fry Glass Co.
Pattern: Unidentified
Color: Amber
Size: 3"
Value: $25.00

Company: **Imperial Glass Co.**
Pattern: **Twin #153** (pillar flute)
Color: Amber
Size: 4⅜"
Value: $16.00

Company: **New Martinsville Glass Co.**
Pattern: **#453, 2-lite**
Color: Amber
Size: 5½"
Value: $45.00

AMBER

Company: **New Martinsville Glass Co.**
Pattern: **Moondrops #37/2 ("Wings")**
Color: Amber
Size: 5"
Value: $20.00

Company: **New Martinsville Glass Co.**
Pattern: **Radiance #42**
Color: Amber
Size: 8"
Value: $95.00

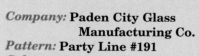

Company: **Paden City Glass
            Manufacturing Co.**
Pattern: **Party Line #191**
Color: Amber
Size: 4¼"
Value: $10.00

Company: **Paden City Glass Manufacturing Co.**
Pattern: **Crow's Foot Round #890, Oriental**
Garden etch, 2-lite
Color: Amber
Size: 5¼"
Value: $40.00

Company: **U.S. Glass Co./Tiffin**
Pattern: **Brocade #326, Flower Garden**
with Butterflies etch
Color: Amber
Size: 8½"
Value: $40.00

AMBER

Company: **Westmoreland Glass Co.**
Pattern: **English Hobnail #555**
Color: Amber
Size: 3¾"
Value: $12.50

Company: **Westmoreland Glass Co.**
Pattern: **Lotus #1921**
Color: Amber
Size: 4"
Value: $15.00

Amethyst

Company: **Cambridge Glass Co.**
Pattern: **Mt. Vernon #38**
Color: Heatherbloom
Size: 13¼"
Value: $1,000.00

Company: **Cambridge Glass Co.**
Pattern: **Decagon #646, Apple Blossom etch #744**
Color: Heatherbloom
Size: 5"
Value: $125.00

Company: **Cambridge Glass Co.**
Pattern: **#647, 2-lite**
Color: Heatherbloom
Size: 5½"
Value: $75.00

Company: **Cambridge Glass Co.**
Pattern: **Decagon #878**
Color: Amethyst (w/Charleton decoration)
Size: 3¾"
Value: $100.00

Company: **Cambridge Glass Co.**
Pattern: **#2798**
Color: Mulberry
Size: 2¾"
Value: $40.00

Company: **Cambridge Glass Co.**
Pattern: **Tulip #1438**
        (candle insert for vases)
Color: Sun-colored Amethyst
Size: 2¾"
Value: $25.00

AMETHYST

Company: **Central Glass Works**
Pattern: **Harding #2000**
Color: Orchid
Size: 3⅛"
Value: $30.00

Company: **Consolidated Lamp &**
Glass Co.
Pattern: **Catalonian #1124 (aka Old**
Spanish), etch #1124
Color: Amethyst Wash
Size: 3"
Value: $35.00

Company: **Dell Glass Co.**
Pattern: **Tulip**
Color: Purple
Size: 3¾"
Value: $25.00

Company: **Dell Glass Co.**
Pattern: **Tulip**
Color: Purple
Size: 3⅜"
Value: $45.00

AMETHYST

AMETHYST

Company: **Fostoria Glass Co.**
Pattern: **#2324, Mt. Vernon etch #277**
Color: Orchid
Size: 3"
Value: $30.00

Company: **Fostoria Glass Co.**
Pattern: **#2393, 3-toe**
Color: Wisteria
Size: 2¼"
Value: $40.00

Company: **Hazel-Atlas Glass Co.**
Pattern: **Star #930**
Color: Moroccan Amethyst
Size: 1¼"
Value: $50.00

Company: **Morgantown Glass Works**
Pattern: **Majesty #7662, Nasreen etch #776**
Color: Alexandrite
Size: 4"
Value: $150.00

AMETHYST

Company: **New Martinsville Glass Co.**
Pattern: **Moondrops #37**
Color: Amethyst
Size: 2½"
Value: $20.00

Company: **Pairpoint Corporation**
Pattern: **#1600, "Grape" Etched**
Color: Purple
Size: 16"
Value: $750.00

Company: **Utility Glass Works**
Pattern: **Cambodia Line**
Color: Amethyst
Size: 3¼"
Value: $40.00

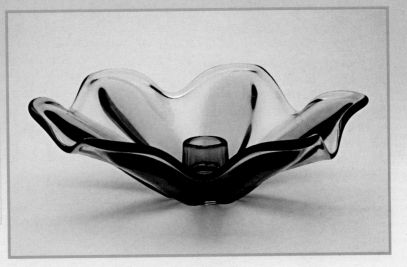

Company: **Viking Glass Co.**
Pattern: **Epic #1409**
Color: Amethyst
Size: 2½"
Value: $15.00

Company: **U.S. Glass Co.**
Pattern: **#18**
Color: Twilite
Size: 2"
Value: $22.50

Company: **U.S. Glass Co.**
Pattern: **Hobnail #518**
Color: Plum
Size: 3½"
Value: $25.00

AMETHYST

Black

Company: Cambridge Glass Co.
Pattern: #68
Color: Black
Size: 10"
Value: $40.00

Company: Cambridge Glass Co.
Pattern: #437
Color: Ebony
Size: 9½"
Value: $40.00

Company: Cambridge Glass Co.
Pattern: Imperial Hunt Scene
#638, 3-lite
Color: Black (gold encrusted)
Size: 6"
Value: $150.00

Company: **Dalzell Viking**
Pattern: **Princess Plaza #5515, 3-lite**
Color: Black (w/pink inserts)
Size: 6¾"
Value: $25.00

Company: **Cambridge Glass Co.**
Pattern: **Cherub #1191**
Color: Ebony
Size: 6"
Value: $400.00

Company: **Dalzell Viking**
Pattern: **Flame, "Squirrel" #8566**
Color: Black
Size: 6½"
Value: $20.00

BLACK

Company: **Libbey Glass Co.**
Pattern: **Worthington #4084**
          (reissued by Viking as #8423)
Color: Black Amethyst
Size: 4¼"
Value: $12.00

Company: **Diamond Glass-ware Co.**
Pattern: **#99**
Color: Black (silver decorated)
Size: 3"
Value: $22.50

Company: **Diamond Glass-ware Co.**
Pattern: **Gothic #716**
Color: Black
Size: 3½"
Value: $25.00

Company: **Diamond Glass-ware Co.**
Pattern: **#625**
Color: Black
Size: 3¾"
Value: $15.00

BLACK

Company: **Diamond Glass-ware Co.**
Pattern: **Trumpet Shape**
Color: Black (w/gold decoration)
Size: 9"
Value: $25.00

Company: **Duncan and Miller Glass Co.**
Pattern: **#16**
Color: Black (w/silver decoration)
Size: 6¼"
Value: $40.00

Company: **Fenton Art Glass Co.**
Pattern: **#2318**
Color: Black
Size: 6"
Value: $45.00

Company: **Fostoria Glass Co.**
Pattern: **Trindle #2383**
Color: Ebony
Size: 4"
Value: $30.00

Company: **Fostoria Glass Co.**
Pattern: **Scroll #2395**
Color: Ebony
Size: 3⅜"
Value: $25.00

BLACK

Company: **Fostoria Glass Co.**
Pattern: **Scroll #2395½**
Color: Ebony
Size: 5"
Value: $22.50

Company: **H.C. Fry Glass Co.**
Pattern: **Unidentified**
Color: Ebony
Size: 3"
Value: $25.00

Company: **McKee Glass Co.**
Pattern: **Scalloped Edge #157**
Color: Black
Size: 2"
Value: $25.00

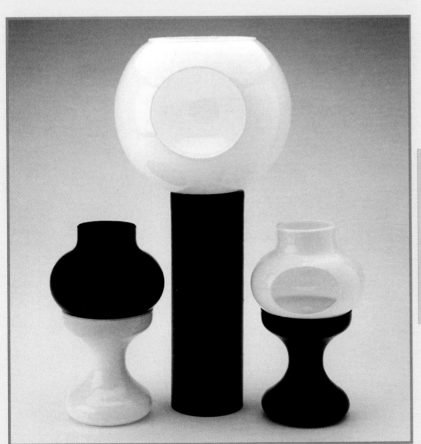

Company: **Morgantown Glass Works**
Pattern: **"Winken" #1214 and**
   "Blinken" #1213 (left & right)
   "Peek-a-boo" style matchmate
   candlelights; **"Royal" #1304**
   (center) pedestal candlelight
Color: Black w/white
Size: 8" (matchmates), 15" (pedestal)
Value: $45.00 (matchmates),
   $75.00 (pedestal)

Company: **Morgantown Guild**
Pattern: **Moonscape #3045**
Color: Steel bowl, Mist base
Size: 16"
Value: $145.00

Company: **New Martinsville
Glass Co.**
Pattern: **#10**
Color: Black
Size: 3"
Value: $10.00

Company: **New Martinsville Glass Co.**
Pattern: **"Addie" #18**
Color: Black
Size: 3½"
Value: $20.00

Company: **Paden City Glass Manufacturing Co.**
Pattern: **Crow's Foot #412, Ardith etch**
Color: Black
Size: 4¾"
Value: $75.00

Company: L.E. Smith Glass Co.
Pattern: Loop Handle #408
Color: Black
Size: 3¼"
Value: $10.00

Company: L.E. Smith Glass Co.
Pattern: Mt. Pleasant Double Shield
Color: Black
Size: 2¼"
Value: $15.00

Company: **L.E. Smith Glass Co.**
Pattern: **Mt. Pleasant Double Shield**
Color: Black
Size: 3"
Value: $60.00

Company: **U.S. Glass Co.**
Pattern: **Ribbed #18**
Color: Black
Size: 2"
Value: $12.00

BLACK

Company: **Westmoreland Glass Co.**
Pattern: **Octagon Candle #1211-2**
Color: Black
Size: 3½"
Value: $15.00

Company: **U.S. Glass Co.**
Pattern: **Deerwood #101**
Color: Black (w/gold)
Size: 2½"
Value: $65.00

Company: **Cambridge Glass Co.**
Pattern: **Star**
Color: Moonlight Blue
Size: 4" wide
Value: $10.00

Company: **Cambridge Glass Co.**
Pattern: **Doric Column #65**
Color: Azurite
Size: 9½"
Value: $85.00

Company: **Cambridge Glass Co.**
Pattern: **#437, Etch #708**
Color: Royal Blue
Size: 9½"
Value: $75.00 each

Company: **Cambridge Glass Co.**
Pattern: **Diane #646**
Color: Moonlight Blue
Size: 5"
Value: $175.00

Company: **Cambridge Glass Co.**
Pattern: **Decagon #646**
Color: Royal Blue (w/gold wildflower)
Size: 5"
Value: $400.00

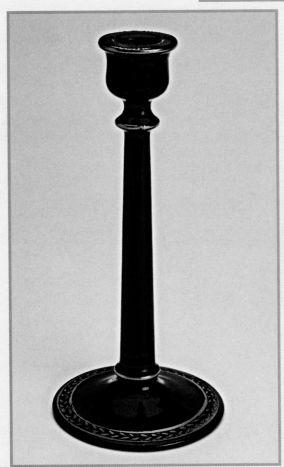

Company: **Cambridge Glass Co.**
Pattern: **#1273, Laurel Leaf #610 decoration**
Color: Cobalt No. 2 (w/goldband overlay)
Size: 9"
Value: $40.00

BLUE

Company: **Cambridge Glass Co.**
Pattern: **#1355 and #1356**
       (w/bobeche & prisms)
Color: Moonlight Blue
Size: 6⅞"
Value: $100.00 (candlestick only)
       $300.00 (complete set)

BLUE

Company: **Cambridge Glass Co.**
Pattern: **#1442** (w/bobeches)
Color: Royal Blue
Size: 11"
Value: $400.00

Company: **Cambridge Glass Co.**
Pattern: **#1545**
Color: Moonlight Blue
Size: 5½"
Value: $100.00

Company: **Cambridge Glass Co.**
Pattern: **Moderne**
Color: Moonlight Blue
Size: 2¾"
Value: $35.00

BLUE

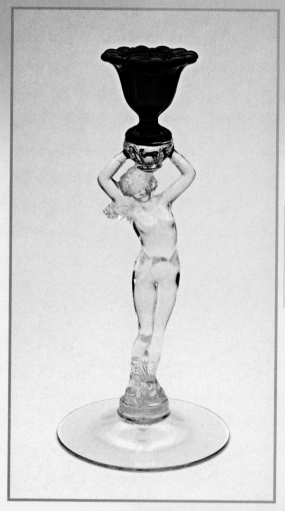

Company: **Cambridge Glass Co.**
Pattern: **Statuesque #3011**
Color: Royal Blue (candle cup)
Size: 9"
Value: $250.00

Company: **Cambridge Glass Co.**
Pattern: **Unidentified**
Color: Azurite (w/gold trim)
Size: 9½"
Value: $50.00 each (candlevase)
$40.00 (bowl)

Company: **Central Glass Works**
Pattern: **#2000**
Color: Blue
Size: 7"
Value: $25.00

Company: **Duncan and Miller Glass Co.**
Pattern: **"Venetian" #5**
Color: Cobalt
Size: 6"
Value: $75.00

Company: **Duncan and Miller Glass Co.**
Pattern: **#50**
Color: Opalescent Blue
Size: 3"
Value: $25.00

BLUE

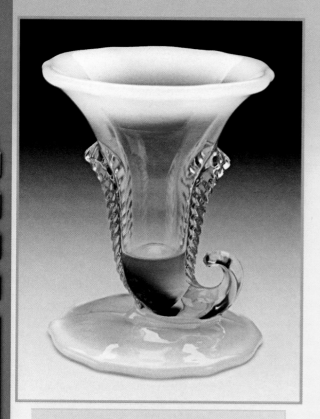

Company: **Duncan and Miller Glass Co.**
Pattern: **"Three Feathers" #117**
Color: Blue Opalescent
Size: 4¼"
Value: $40.00

Company: **Duncan and Miller Glass Co.**
Pattern: **Festive #155/60**
Color: Aqua
Size: 5½"
Value: $50.00

Company: **Duncan and Miller
Glass Co.**
Pattern: **Terrace #111**
Color: Blue
Size: 4"
Value: $75.00

Company: **Fenton Art Glass Co.**
Pattern: **#314**
Color: Celeste Blue Stretch
Size: 1½"
Value: $20.00

Company: **Fenton Art Glass Co.**
Pattern: **#848, 9-petal**
Color: Royal Blue
Size: 1⅝"
Value: $18.00

BLUE

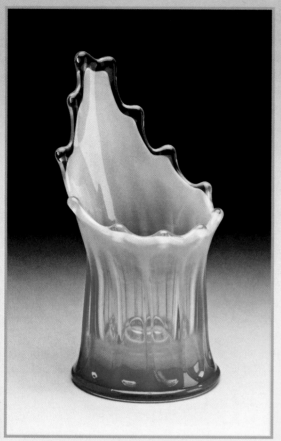

Company: **Fostoria Glass Co.**
Pattern: **Fairfax #2375½**
Color: Azure
Size: 2⅜"
Value: $20.00

Company: **Fostoria Glass Co.**
Pattern: **Heirloom #1515/311** (candlevase)
Color: Blue Opalescent
Size: 9"
Value: $75.00

Company: **Fostoria Glass Co.**
Pattern: **Fairfax #2375½,**
           Versailles etch #278
Color: Azure
Size: 2⅝"
Value: $35.00 (candle), $135.00
        (bowl), $75.00 (frog)

Company: Fostoria Glass Co.
Pattern: **#2484** (w/eight prisms)
Color: Lustre
Size: 7¾"
Value: $75.00

Company: **Fostoria Glass Co.**
Pattern: **Baroque #2496**
Color: Azure
Size: 3⅞"
Value: $30.00

BLUE

Company: **Fostoria Glass Co.**
Pattern: **Flame Duo #2545**
Color: Azure
Size: 6⅞"
Value: $65.00

Company: **Fostoria Glass Co.**
Pattern: **#2324 Columbine**
              Variant Cut
Color: Blue
Size: 3"
Value: $25.00

Company: **Fostoria Glass Co.**
Pattern: **#2375**
Color: Blue (w/silver decorations)
Size: 3½"
Value: $22.50

Company: **Fostoria Glass Co.**
Pattern: **#2324**
Color: Blue (w/gold decorations)
Size: 12"
Value: $50.00

Company: **Fostoria Glass Co.**
Pattern: **Fairfax #2375**
Color: Azure
Size: 3⅜"
Value: $25.00 (plain), $35.00
(w/pressed, dried flowers)

Company: **Fostoria Glass Co.**
Pattern: **Fairfax #2375½,**
Oakwood etch #290
Color: Azure
Size: 2⅜"
Value: $50.00

BLUE

Company: **Hazel-Atlas Glass Co.**
Pattern: **Royal Lace Ruffled**
Color: Ritz Blue
Size: 2¼"
Value: $225.00

Company: **Imperial Glass Co.**
Pattern: **Olive #134**
Color: Viennese Blue
Size: 2½"
Value: $15.00

Company: **A.H. Heisey & Co.**
Pattern: **Old Sandwich #1404**
Color: Cobalt
Size: 6"
Value: $250.00

Company: **Imperial Glass Co.**
Pattern: **Candlewick #400/86,**
         "Mushroom"
Color: Blue
Size: 2"
Value: $50.00

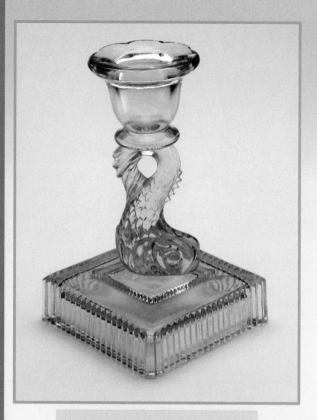

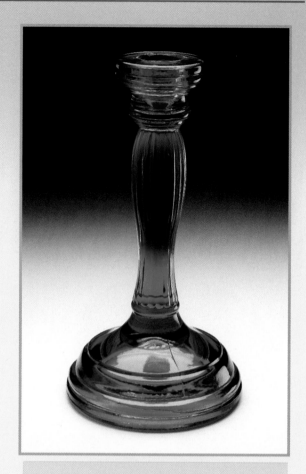

Company: **Imperial Glass Co.**
Pattern: **Empire Dolphin #779**
Color: Viennese Blue
Size: 5"
Value: $25.00

Company: **Indiana Glass Co.**
Pattern: **Wedgewood #4, Tiara-Duchess #10009**
Color: Blue
Size: 8⅛"
Value: $22.50

Company: **Indiana Glass Co.**
Pattern: **#603**
Color: Blue/White (w/silver)
Size: 4"
Value: $25.00

BLUE

Company: **Indiana Glass Co.**
Pattern: **Willow/Oleander**
                #1008, 2-lite
Color: Flashed Blue
Size: 5½"
Value: $25.00

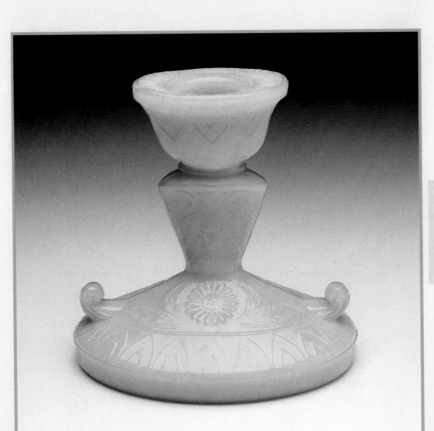

Company: **McKee Glass Co.**
Pattern: **Autumn**
Color: Poudre Blue
Size: 4¼"
Value: $100.00

BLUE

BLUE

Company: **Morgantown Glass Works**
Pattern: **Federal #9935, Barton Stem**
Color: Peacock Blue
Size: 3¾"
Value: $20.00

Company: **Morgantown Glass Works**
Pattern: **Classic #88**
Color: Peacock Blue
Size: 4⅝"
Value: $20.00

Company: **Morgantown Glass Works**
Pattern: **Golf Ball #7643** (torch candle)
Color: Ritz Blue
Size: 6"
Value: $175.00

Company: **Morgantown Glass Works**
Pattern: **Majesty #7662**
Color: Ritz Blue (w/gold "Sparta"
      decoration)
Size: 4"
Value: $100.00 (plain),
       $150.00 (w/decoration)

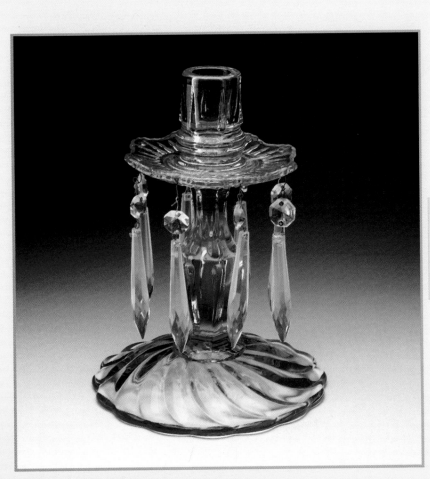

Company: **New Martinsville Glass Co.**
Pattern: **Radiance #42**
Color: Colonial Blue
Size: 8"
Value: $150.00

Company: **New Martinsville Glass Co.**
Pattern: **Janice (flame) #4585**
Color: Colonial Blue
Size: 5½"
Value: $75.00

Company: **Paden City Glass**
Manufacturing Co.
Pattern: **Largo #220**
Color: Copen Blue
Size: 5"
Value: $40.00

Company: **Paden City Glass Manufacturing Co.**
Pattern: **#300 Archaic, Cupid etch**
Color: Blue
Size: 1⅞"
Value: $175.00

Company: **L.E. Smith Glass Co.**
Pattern: **Mt. Pleasant Double Shield #600/4**
Color: Cobalt
Size: 4½" x 5¾"
Value: $25.00

BLUE

BLUE

Company: **Sinclaire & Co.**
Pattern: **#12928**
Color: Isis Blue
Size: 3½"
Value: $125.00

Company: **U.S. Glass Co.**
Pattern: **#76**
Color: Blue (decorated)
Size: 8"
Value: $50.00

Company: **U.S. Glass Co.**
Pattern: **#94**
Color: Sky Blue
Size: 1½"
Value: $15.00

Company: **U.S. Glass Co.**
Pattern: **#300**
Color: Royal Blue
Size: 9"
Value: $40.00

BLUE

Company: **U.S. Glass Co./Tiffin**
Pattern: **#6125**
Color: Blue
Size: 4¾"
Value: $100.00

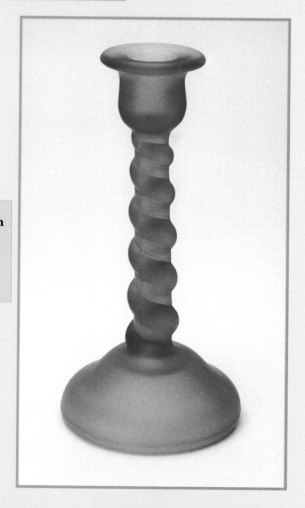

Company: **U.S. Glass Co./Tiffin**
Pattern: **Twisted**
Color: Blue (satin)
Size: 9"
Value: $25.00

Company: **Viking Glass Co.**
Pattern: **Epic #1196**
Color: Blunique
Size: 1¾"
Value: $25.00

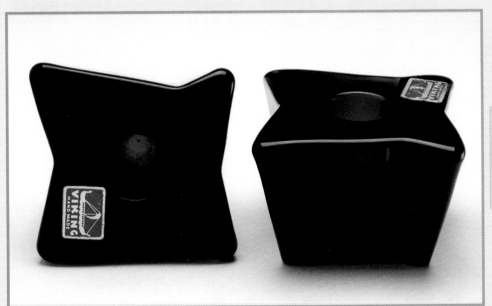

Company: **Viking Glass Co.**
Pattern: **Astra/Epic #6112**
Color: Blunique
Size: 2"
Value: $12.00

BLUE

Company: **Anchor Hocking Glass Co.**
Pattern: **Bubble**
Color: Crystal
Size: 2"
Value: $12.50

Company: **Anchor Hocking Glass Co.**
Pattern: **Queen Mary #982**
(prismatic line #982),
2-lite
Color: Crystal
Size: 4" x 4"
Value: $10.00

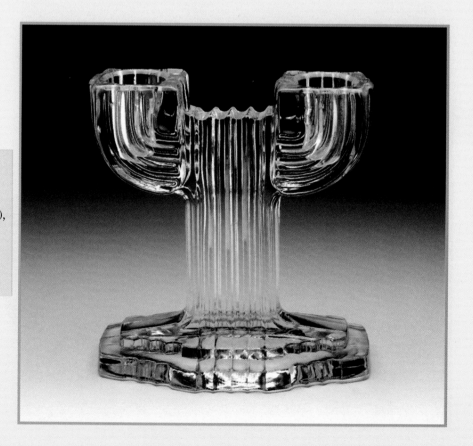

CRYSTAL

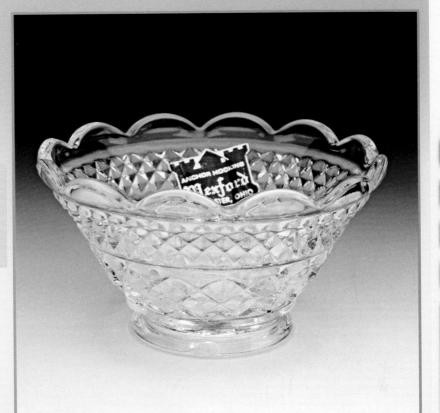

Company: **Anchor Hocking Glass Co.**
Pattern: **Wexford**
Color: Crystal
Size: 4"
Value: $20.00

Company: **Anchor Hocking Glass Co.**
Pattern: **#982**
Color: Crystal
Size: 4½"
Value: $8.00

Company: **Beaumont Co.**
Pattern: **Triple Candle**
Color: Satinized Crystal
Size: 4"
Value: $40.00

Company: **Blenko Glass Co.**
Pattern: **Line #990A**
Color: Crystal
Size: 2"
Value: $6.00

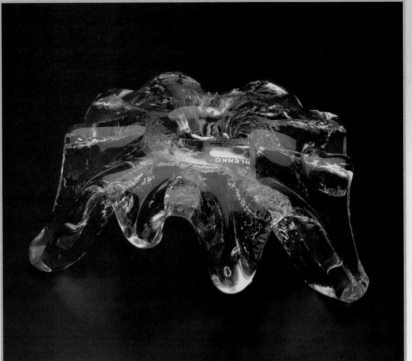

Company: **Blenko Glass Co.**
Pattern: **Line #9516**
Color: Crystal
Size: 2"
Value: $20.00

Company: **Cambridge Glass Co.**
Pattern: **Dolphin #50** (w/extender
          for hurricane shades)
Color: Crystal
Size: 7¾"
Value: $85.00

CRYSTAL

Company: **Cambridge Glass Co.**
Pattern: **"Dolphin" (Fish) #67,**
                2-lite
Color: Crystal
Size: 5"
Value: $50.00

Company: **Cambridge Glass Co.**
Pattern: **Caprice #74, 3-lite**
Color: Crystal
Size: 4"
Value: $35.00

Company: **Cambridge Glass Co.**
Pattern: **#704 etch "Many Windows"**
            #227½ (candle)
Color: Crystal
Size: 1½"
Value: $10.00

Company: **Cambridge Glass Co.**
Pattern: **Martha #495, Rosepoint**
            etch, 2-lite
Color: Crystal
Size: 5½"
Value: $65.00

CRYSTAL

Company: **Cambridge Glass Co.**
Pattern: **Pristine #500, Wildflower etch**
Color: Crystal
Size: 6½"
Value: $65.00

Company: **Cambridge Glass Co.**
Pattern: **Virginian #502, Diane etch #752, 2-lite**
Color: Crystal
Size: 5½"
Value: $50.00

Company: **Cambridge Glass Co.**
Pattern: **Pristine #510**
Color: Crystal
Size: 2⅜"
Value: $18.00

Company: **Cambridge Glass Co.**
Pattern: **#627 candle, Adonis cut
#720**
Color: Crystal
Size: 3¾"
Value: $35.00

CRYSTAL

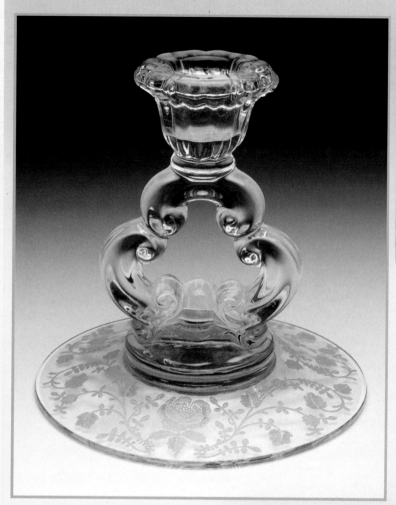

Company: **Cambridge Glass Co.**
Pattern: **Roselyn, #646 "Keyhole" design**
Color: Crystal
Size: 5"
Value: $25.00

Company: **Cambridge Glass Co.**
Pattern: **#647, Elaine etch #752,**
       "Keyhole" design,
       2-lite
Color: Crystal
Size: 5½" x 8" (across top)
Value: $45.00

CRYSTAL

Company: Cambridge Glass Co.
Pattern: "Ram's Head/Cornucopia"
#657, Adonis cut, #720,
2-lite
Color: Crystal
Size: 5½"
Value: $100.00

Company: Cambridge Glass Co.
Pattern: Decagon #878, "Majestic"
etch #732
Color: Crystal
Size: 4"
Value: $22.50

CRYSTAL

Company: **Cambridge Glass Co.**
Pattern: **Cherub #1191**
Color: Crystal
Size: 6"
Value: $150.00

Company: **Cambridge Glass Co.**
Pattern: **Everglade #1155** (goes
w/#1150, 12½" console
bowl)
Color: Crystal
Size: 2¼"
Value: $15.00

CRYSTAL

Company: **Cambridge Glass Co.**
Pattern: **Triple Candle #1307**
Color: Crystal
Size: 5"
Value: $25.00

Company: **Cambridge Glass Co.**
Pattern: **Triple Candle #1307,**
            Chintz etch #D/995
Color: Crystal
Size: 5½"
Value: $50.00

Company: **Cambridge Glass Co.**
Pattern: **Triple Candle #1307,**
          Marjorie etch
Color: Crystal
Size: 6½"
Value: $150.00

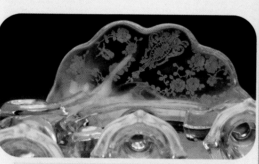

Company: **Cambridge Glass Co.**
Pattern: **Rosepoint #1338, 3-lite,**
          (Caprice style but not
          considered to be Caprice)
Color: Crystal
Size: 6"
Value: $75.00

CRYSTAL

Company: **Cambridge Glass Co.**
Pattern: **Rosepoint #1338, 3-lite,**
(Caprice style but not
considered to be Caprice)
Color: Crystal (w/gold)
Size: 6"
Value: $110.00

Company: **Cambridge Glass Co.**
Pattern: **Caprice #1357**
(w/#1438 arm),
2 vases, 3-lite
Color: Crystal
Size: 7"
Value: $150.00 as shown

CRYSTAL

Company: **Cambridge Glass Co.**
Pattern: **Tally Ho #1402/80,**
 Elaine etch #762
Color: Crystal
Size: 6"
Value: $65.00

Company: **Cambridge Glass Co.**
Pattern: **Flower Frog #1505** (w/center candlestick)
 Flower Frog #1504 (w/center candlestick)
Color: Crystal
Size: 5¾" (#1505), 7" (#1504)
Value: $15.00; $20.00

Company: **Cambridge Glass Co.**
Pattern: **Epergnette #1580**
(needs ball vase
middle #78)
Color: Crystal
Size: 5⅜"
Value: $25.00

Company: **Cambridge Glass Co.**
Pattern: **#1604 Chantilly, #772 etch**
Color: Crystal
Size: 2½" (as shown) 10" (w/globe)
Value: $60.00

CRYSTAL

Company: **Cambridge Glass Co.**
Pattern: **Dolphin #1612** (base), **Wildflower etch #1614** (hurricane shade)
Color: Crystal (w/gold decoration)
Size: 16"
Value: $375.00

Company: **Cambridge Glass Co.**
Pattern: **Dolphin #1612** (base), **Chantilly etch #1615** (hurricane lamp)
Color: Crystal
Size: 16"
Value: $300.00

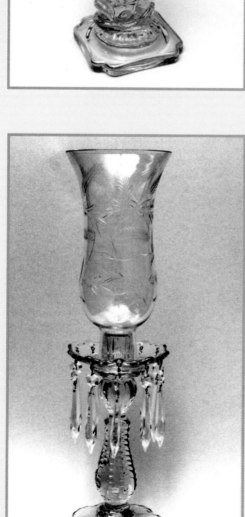

Company: **Cambridge Glass Co.**
Pattern: **Cut Harvest #1613**
Color: Crystal
Size: 17½"
Value: $250.00

Company: Cambridge Glass Co.
Pattern: #3121 Wildflower
Color: Crystal (gold encrusted)
Size: 7"
Value: $90.00

Company: Cambridge Glass Co.
Pattern: Gadroon #3500/108
Elaine etch #762
Color: Crystal (gold encrusted)
Size: 2½"
Value: $35.00

Company: Cambridge Glass Co.
Pattern: #3900/67, Elaine etch
#762 (shade)
Color: Crystal
Size: 10" (w/shade)
Value: $110.00

CRYSTAL

Company: **Cambridge Glass Co.**
Pattern: **Corinth #3900/68,** (can be turned up to use as compote)
Color: Crystal
Size: 5"
Value: $22.50

CRYSTAL

Company: **Cambridge Glass Co.**
Pattern: **Cascade #4000/67**
Color: Crystal
Size: 4½"
Value: $20.00

Company: Cambridge Glass Co.
Pattern: Candelabrum parts
Color: Crystal
Size: 16"
Value: Peg nappy, $10.00 each;
          peg vase, $15.00 each;
          trindle holder, $20.00 each;
          base #628, 3¾", $10.00

Company: Cambridge Glass Co.
Pattern: Rosepoint
          Candelabrum parts
Color: Crystal
Size: 16"
Value: Peg nappy, $100.00 each;
          peg vase, $125.00 each;
          trindle holder, $25.00;
          base #628, 3¾", $30.00

CRYSTAL

Company: **Central Glass Works**
Pattern: **Chippendale** (miniature)
Color: Crystal
Size: 4¼"
Value: $15.00

CRYSTAL

Company: **Colony Glassware**
Pattern: **Whitehall**
Color: Crystal
Size: 2"
Value: $4.00

Company: **Duncan and Miller Glass Co.**
Pattern: **First Love #1-4** (hurricane lamp candelabrum w/prisms)
Color: Crystal
Size: 15"
Value: $150.00

Company: **Duncan and Miller Glass Co.**
Pattern: **#4, 4-lite**
Color: Crystal
Size: 10"
Value: $125.00

CRYSTAL

Company: **Duncan and Miller Glass Co.**
Pattern: **Early American Sandwich #41-125, 2-lite**
Color: Crystal
Size: 6"
Value: $35.00

Company: **Duncan and Miller Glass Co.**
Pattern: **#65, 2-lite**
Color: Crystal
Size: 12"
Value: $150.00

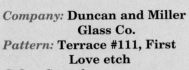

Company: **Duncan and Miller Glass Co.**
Pattern: **Terrace #111, First Love etch**
Color: Crystal
Size: 4"
Value: $30.00

CRYSTAL

Company: **Duncan and Miller Glass Co.**
Pattern: **Canterbury #115**
Color: Crystal
Size: 6"
Value: $25.00

Company: **Duncan and Miller Glass Co.**
Pattern: **Canterbury Line #115,**
          Magnolia design
Color: Crystal
Size: 3"
Value: $20.00

Company: **Duncan and Miller Glass**
          Co.; U.S. Glass Co./Tiffin
Pattern: **Murano #125** (candle/flower
          arranger)
Color: Crystal
Size: 2½"
Value: $25.00

Company: **Duncan and Miller Glass Co.**
Pattern: **Teardrop #301**
Color: Crystal
Size: 4½"
Value: $35.00

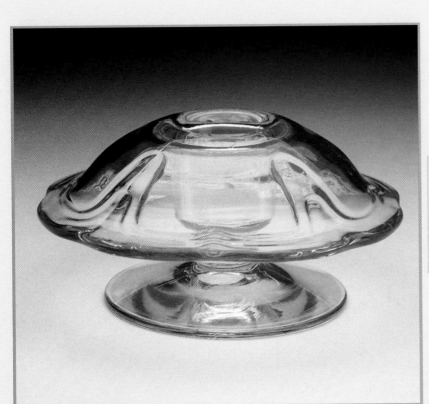

Company: **Duncan and Miller Glass Co.**
Pattern: **Puritan**
Color: Crystal
Size: 2"
Value: $20.00

CRYSTAL

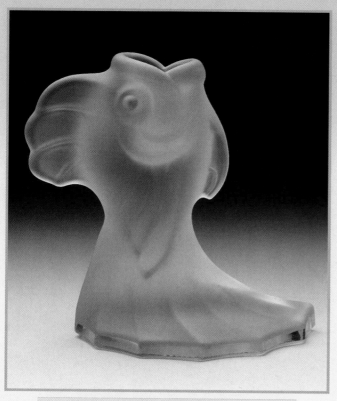

CRYSTAL

Company: **Federal Glass Co.**
Pattern: **#2758 Petal**
Color: Crystal
Size: 2"
Value: $5.00

Company: **Duncan and Miller Glass Co.**
Pattern: **Tropical Fish**
Color: Crystal (frosted)
Size: 5"
Value: $500.00

Company: **Federal Glass Co.**
Pattern: **Pioneer #2806½**
Color: Crystal
Size: 1¾"
Value: $8.00

CRYSTAL

Company: **Fostoria Glass Co.**
Pattern: **Coronation**
Color: Crystal
Size: 6" or 8"
Value: $30.00 each

Company: **Fostoria Glass Co.**
Pattern: **#2324**
Color: Crystal (w/silver overlay)
Size: 3"
Value: $15.00

Company: **Fostoria Glass Co.**
Pattern: **Fairfax #2375,**
            June etch #279
Color: Crystal
Size: 3¼"
Value: $20.00

Company: **Fostoria Glass Co.**
Pattern: **Colony Glassware #2412**
Color: Crystal
Size: 7"
Value: $30.00

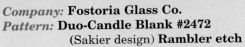

Company: **Fostoria Glass Co.**
Pattern: **Duo-Candle Blank #2472**
(Sakier design) **Rambler etch**
Color: Crystal
Size: 5"
Value: $32.50

Company: **Fostoria Glass Co.**
Pattern: **#2484 Trindle**
Color: Crystal
Size: 9⅛"
Value: $80.00

CRYSTAL

Company: **Fostoria Glass Co.**
Pattern: **Baroque #2496, Navarre etch #327**
Color: Crystal
Size: 3⅞"
Value: $28.00

Company: **Fostoria Glass Co.**
Pattern: **Baroque #2496, Corsage etch #325**
Color: Crystal
Size: 5¾"
Value: $50.00

Company: **Fostoria Glass Co.**
Pattern: **Sunray #2510**
Color: Crystal
Size: 3¼"
Value: $18.00

Company: **Fostoria Glass Co.**
Pattern: **Glacier #2510**
Color: Crystal (w/frost)
Size: 3¼" x 4½"
Value: $18.00

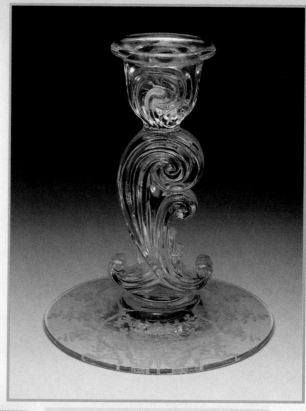

Company: **Fostoria Glass Co.**
Pattern: **"Nocturne" #2527**
Color: Crystal
Size: 8½"
Value: $35.00

Company: **Fostoria Glass Co.**
Pattern: **#2535, Corsage etch #325**
Color: Crystal
Size: 5½"
Value: $40.00

Company: **Fostoria Glass Co.**
Pattern: **Quadrangle #2546**
Color: Crystal
Size: 4¾"
Value: $65.00

CRYSTAL

Company: **Fostoria Glass Co.**
Pattern: **Coronet #2560, Mayflower etch #332**
Color: Crystal
Size: 4⅜" x 4¼"
Value: $35.00

Company: **Fostoria Glass Co.**
Pattern: **Coronet #2560½, Willomere etch #333**
Color: Crystal
Size: 4"
Value: $35.00

Company: **Fostoria Glass Co.**
Pattern: **Myriad #2592**
Color: Crystal
Size: 3½"
Value: $25.00

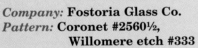

CRYSTAL

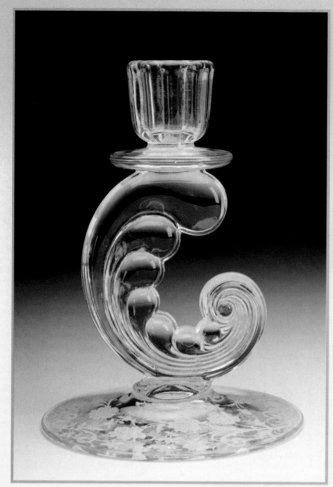

Company: **Fostoria Glass Co.**
Pattern: **Plume #2594, Buttercup etch #340**
Color: Crystal
Size: 5¾"
Value: $25.00

CRYSTAL

Company: **Fostoria Glass Co.**
Pattern: **Wistar #2620**
Color: Crystal
Size: 4"
Value: $18.00

Company: **Fostoria Glass Co.**
Pattern: **Century #2630, Camelia etch #344**
Color: Crystal
Size: 4½"
Value: $17.50

Company: **Fostoria Glass Co.**
Pattern: **Century Duo #2630**
Color: Crystal
Size: 6¾"
Value: $25.00

CRYSTAL

Company: **Fostoria Glass Co.**
Pattern: **Plume #2636**
        (Sakier design)
Color: Crystal
Size: 9¾"
Value: $40.00

Company: **Fostoria Glass Co.**
Pattern: **#2639 Duo** (Sakier design)
Color: Crystal
Size: 9¾"
Value: $75.00

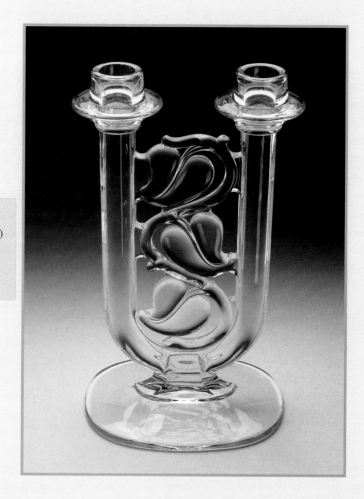

Company: **Fostoria Glass Co.**
Pattern: **Garden Center #2640**
Color: Crystal
Size: 7"
Value: $125.00

Company: **Fostoria Glass Co.**
Pattern: **#2668/459**
Color: Crystal
Size: 2½"
Value: $15.00, $25.00 (w/hurricane
        lamp shade, not shown)

CRYSTAL

Company: **Fostoria Glass Co.**
Pattern: **Sonata Duo #6023,**
Romance Plate etch #341
Color: Crystal
Size: 5½"
Value: $35.00

CRYSTAL

Company: **Hazel-Atlas Glass Co.**
Pattern: **Royal Lace** (rolled edge)
Color: Crystal
Size: 2¼"
Value: $30.00

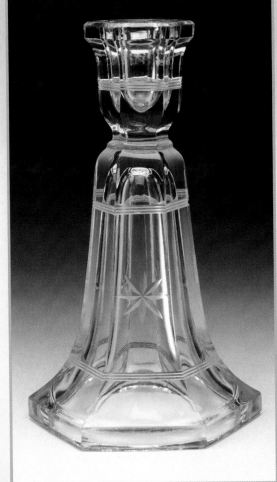

Company: **A.H. Heisey & Co.**
Pattern: **Mercury #112**
Color: Crystal
Size: 3¾"
Value: $20.00

Company: **A.H. Heisey & Co.**
Pattern: **Skirted Panel #33** (w/cut)
Color: Crystal
Size: 9"
Value: $50.00

Company: **A.H. Heisey & Co.**
Pattern: **Cascade #142,**
          Orchid etch #507
Color: Crystal
Size: 7⅜"
Value: $85.00

CRYSTAL

Company: A.H. Heisey & Co.
Pattern: Victorian #1425, 2-lite
Color: Crystal
Size: 5¾"
Value: $75.00

Company: A.H. Heisey & Co.
Pattern: Ridgeleigh #1469½
Color: Crystal
Size: 3"
Value: $20.00

Company: A.H. Heisey & Co.
Pattern: Empire #1471, 3-lite
Color: Crystal
Size: 6⅞"
Value: $225.00

CRYSTAL

Company: **A.H. Heisey & Co.**
Pattern: **Fern #1495, Floral etch #508, 2-lite**
Color: Crystal
Size: 5½"
Value: $50.00

CRYSTAL

Company: **A.H. Heisey & Co.**
Pattern: **Crystolite #1502**
Color: Crystal
Size: 2¼"
Value: $15.00

Company: **A.H. Heisey & Co.**
Pattern: **Crystolite #1503** (w/10" hurricane shade block)
Color: Crystal
Size: 4" x 2½"
Value: $30.00

Company: **A.H. Heisey & Co.**
Pattern: **Crystolite #1503** (w/o hurricane
shade block)
Color: Crystal
Size: 2½"
Value: $18.00

Company: **A.H. Heisey & Co.**
Pattern: **Crystolite #1503, 2-lite**
Color: Crystal
Size: 6"
Value: $50.00

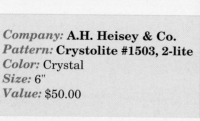

Company: **A.H. Heisey & Co.**
Pattern: **Crystolite #1503¼**
Color: Crystal
Size: 1⅞"
Value: $20.00

Company: **A.H. Heisey & Co.**
Pattern: **Whirlpool #1506 (1938),
 became "Provincial"**
Color: Crystal
Size: 6¼"
Value: $40.00

Company: **A.H. Heisey & Co.**
Pattern: **Waverly #1519 Orchid
 etch #507, 2-lite**
Color: Crystal
Size: 6¼"
Value: $45.00

CRYSTAL

Company: **A.H. Heisey & Co.**
Pattern: **Waverly #1519, Rose etch #515, 3-lite**
Color: Crystal
Size: 7⅛"
Value: $100.00

Company: **A.H. Heisey & Co.**
Pattern: **Lariat #1540** (black out lamp for wartime use), **#5041** (shade)
Color: Crystal
Size: 2½", 7" (with 5" shade)
Value: $400.00

Company: **A.H. Heisey & Co.**
Pattern: **Lariat #1540, 2-lite**
Color: Crystal
Size: 5"
Value: $20.00

CRYSTAL

Company: A.H. Heisey & Co.
Pattern: Lariat #1540, Moonglo cut #980, 2-lite
Color: Crystal
Size: 5"
Value: $30.00

Company: A.H. Heisey & Co.
Pattern: Lariat #1540, 3-lite
Color: Crystal
Size: 6¾"
Value: $30.00

CRYSTAL

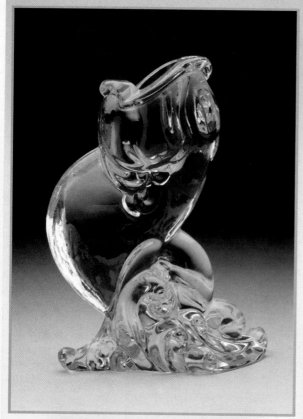

Company: A.H. Heisey & Co.
Pattern: "Fish" #1550
Color: Crystal
Size: 5"
Value: $150.00

Company: A.H. Heisey & Co.
Pattern: Four Leaf #1552
Color: Crystal
Size: 1½"
Value: $30.00

Company: A.H. Heisey & Co.
Pattern: Plantation #1567 (hurricane)
Color: Crystal
Size: 6" (base); 12" (w/shade)
Value: $300.00

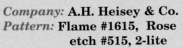

Company: A.H. Heisey & Co.
Pattern: Flame #1615, Rose etch #515, 2-lite
Color: Crystal
Size: 10¼"
Value: $250.00

Company: A.H. Heisey & Co.
Pattern: Block Five #1619 (base) #4233 (peg vase)
Color: Crystal
Size: 2¼" (base); 6" (vase)
Value: $350.00

Company: **A.H. Heisey & Co.**
Pattern: **Cabochon #1951**
Color: Crystal
Size: 1¾"
Value: $20.00

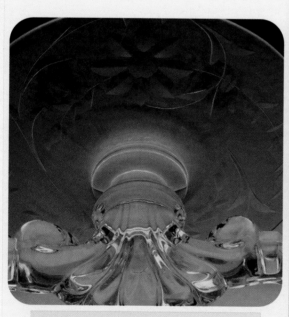

Company: **A.H. Heisey & Co.**
Pattern: **"Trident" #134, Narcissus cut #965**
Color: Crystal
Size: 5¾"
Value: $35.00

Company: A.H. Heisey & Co.
Pattern: Trident #134, Orchid etch
Color: Crystal
Size: 5¾"
Value: $45.00

Company: A.H. Heisey & Co.
Pattern: Trident #134, Rose of
Peace etch #9014
Color: Crystal
Size: 5¾"
Value: $35.00

CRYSTAL

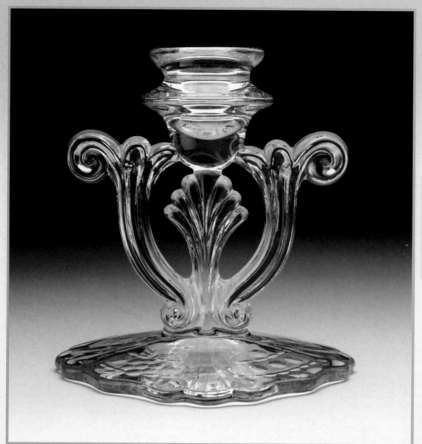

Company: **Imperial Glass Co.**
Pattern: **#148**
Color: Crystal
Size: 5"
Value: $25.00

Company: **Imperial Glass Co.**
Pattern: **Corinthian #280/100.**
  (Photo shows detachable
  base that was to be taken
  off when fire polished.)
Color: Crystal
Size: 4¼"
Value: $30.00

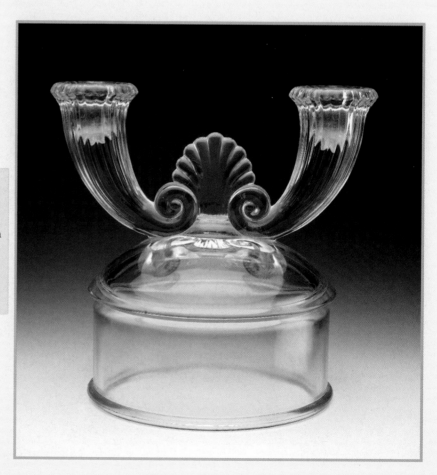

Company: **Imperial Glass Co.**
Pattern: **Candlewick #400/66F**
Color: Crystal
Size: 4"
Value: $65.00

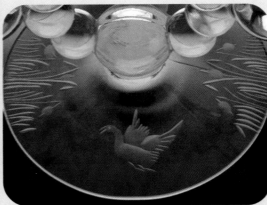

Company: **Imperial Glass Co.**
Pattern: **Candlewick Twin #400/100,**
            Mallard Duck cut (w/reeds)
Color: Crystal
Size: 4½"
Value: $35.00

CRYSTAL

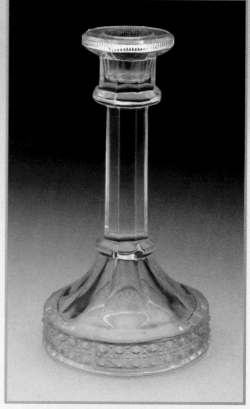

Company: **Imperial Glass Co.**
Pattern: **#607** (candlebowl), **2-lite**
Color: Crystal
Size: 4"
Value: $35.00

Company: **Imperial Glass Co.**
Pattern: **Flute 'N Cane or**
            Amelia, #671 Line
Color: Crystal
Size: 7"
Value: $20.00

Company: **Imperial Glass Co.**
Pattern: **Reeded/"Spun" #701**
Color: Crystal
Size: 2¾", 1½" (separate cup)
Value: $40.00 complete;
            $20.00 insert cup alone

CRYSTAL

Company: **Imperial Glass Co.**
Pattern: **"Double Heart" #753,
3-lite**
Color: Crystal
Size: 6½"
Value: $45.00

Company: **Imperial Glass Co.**
Pattern: **#782, 2-lite**
Color: Crystal
Size: 5¼"
Value: $30.00

Company: **Imperial Glass Co.**
Pattern: **Cathay #5009**
Color: Crystal
Size: 6¾"
Value: $250.00

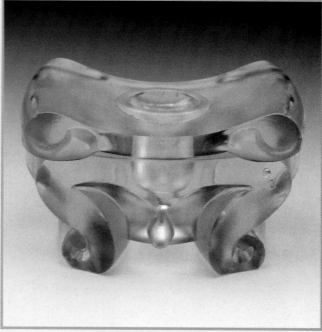

Company: **Imperial Glass Co.**
Pattern: **Cathay Shen #5020/2**
Color: Crystal (frosted)
Size: 2¼"
Value: $90.00

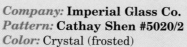

Company: **Imperial Glass Co.**
Pattern: **Cathay Pillow #5013**
Color: Crystal (frosted)
Size: 2½"
Value: $150.00

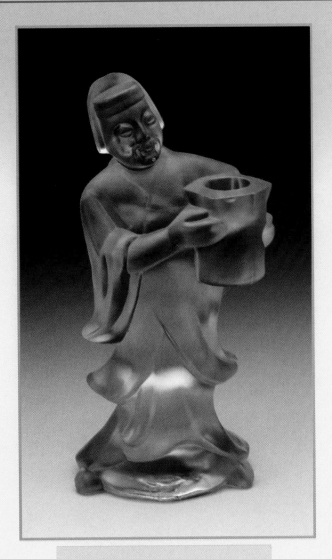

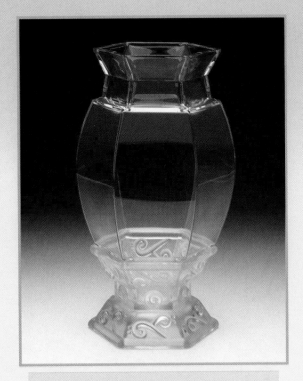

Company: Imperial Glass Co.
Pattern: Cathay Wedding Lamp #5027
Color: Crystal (frosted)
Size: 11½"
Value: $150.00

Company: Imperial Glass Co.
Pattern: Cathay Candle Servant
    (man) #5033
Color: Crystal (frosted)
Size: 9"
Value: $250.00

Company: Imperial Glass Co.
Pattern: Cathay Candle Servant
    (woman) #5034
Color: Crystal (frosted)
Size: 9"
Value: $250.00

CRYSTAL

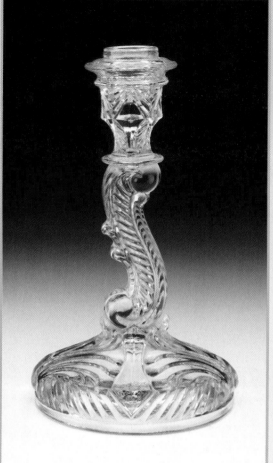

Company: **Indiana Glass Co.**
Pattern: **#303**
Color: Crystal
Size: 8½"
Value: $15.00

Company: **Indiana Glass Co.**
Pattern: **"Block & Rib" #370**
Color: Crystal
Size: 5¼" shown w/two styles of bases
      (above and left)
Value: $15.00 each

CRYSTAL

Company: **Indiana Glass Co.**
Pattern: **Tea Room #600**
Color: Crystal (w/alternating frosted blocks)
Size: 3"
Value: $35.00

Company: **Indiana Glass Co.**
Pattern: **#1006, Roses Silver**
floral overlay, 2-lite
Color: Crystal (w/silver)
Size: 5"
Value: $22.50

Company: **Indiana Glass Co.**
Pattern: **Willow/Oleander #1007,**
2-lite (label "Corsage")
Color: Crystal (gold decorated)
Size: 5⅛"
Value: $22.50

CRYSTAL

Company: **Indiana Glass Co.**
Pattern: **Willow/Oleander**
#1007, 2-lite
Color: Crystal (w/satin)
Size: 5⅛"
Value: $20.00

Company: **Indiana Glass Co.**
Pattern: **Willow/Oleander #1008**
Color: Crystal
Size: 4"
Value: $18.00

CRYSTAL

Company: **Indiana Glass Co.**
Pattern: **Willow/Oleander #1008**
Color: Crystal (w/gold)
Size: 4¼"
Value: $25.00

Company: **Indiana Glass Co.**
Pattern: **Laurel #1010**
Color: Crystal
Size: 4½"
Value: $12.00

CRYSTAL

Company: **Indiana Glass Co.**
Pattern: **Laurel #1010, 2-lite**
Color: Crystal
Size: 5"
Value: $20.00

Company: **Indiana Glass Co.**
Pattern: **"Block & Rib"**
Color: Crystal
Size: 5⅛" (candlesticks), 10" (footed bowl)
Value: $12.50 each (candlesticks), $22.50 (bowl)

Company: **Indiana Glass Co. for Colony
 Glassware**
Pattern: **Epergne, tri-arm** (w/four peg nappies)
Color: Crystal
Size: 9"
Value: $35.00

Company: **Lancaster Glass Co.**
Pattern: **Deco Style**
Color: Crystal
Size: 7⅛"
Value: $25.00

Company: **New Martinsville Glass Co.**
Pattern: **Swan Line #451**
Color: Crystal
Size: 2½"
Value: $30.00

CRYSTAL

Company: New Martinsville Glass Co.
Pattern: #652 Cornucopia
Color: Crystal
Size: 3½"
Value: $15.00

Company: New Martinsville Glass Co.
Pattern: #671 Shell
  (reflector candle/bookend)
Color: Crystal
Size: 6¾"
Value: $40.00

Company: New Martinsville Glass Co.
Pattern: Scroll #1076
Color: Crystal
Size: 2"
Value: $15.00

Company: New Martinsville
Glass Co.
Pattern: Teardrop #4457, Wild
Rose etch, 2-lite
Color: Crystal
Size: 5¼"
Value: $25.00

Company: Paden City Glass
Manufacturing Co.
Pattern: #220 (Largo line)
Color: Crystal
Size: 5¼"
Value: $18.00

CRYSTAL

CRYSTAL

Company: **Paden City Glass Manufacturing Co.**
Pattern: **#215 (Glades line), Spring Orchard etch #545, 2-lite**
Color: Crystal
Size: 5"
Value: $30.00

Company: **Paden City Glass Manufacturing Co.**
Pattern: **#220 (Largo line)**
Color: Crystal (w/silver overlay)
Size: 5¼"
Value: $20.00

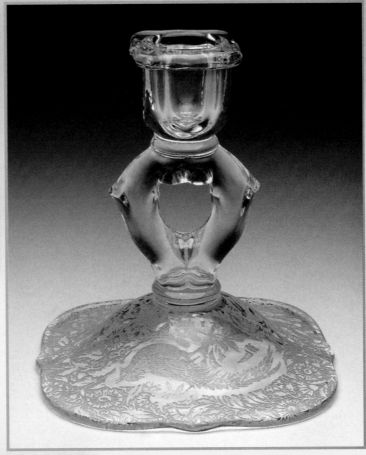

**Company: Paden City Glass
Manufacturing Co.**
Pattern: **"Sasha Bird"/Crow's Foot #412**
Color: Crystal
Size: 5¼"
Value: $35.00

**Company: Paden City Glass
Manufacturing Co.**
Pattern: **#555 line**
Color: Crystal
Size: 6¼"
Value: $20.00

CRYSTAL

Company: **Paden City Glass**
Manufacturing Co.
Pattern: **#555 line, Floral etch**
Color: Crystal
Size: 6¼"
Value: $22.50

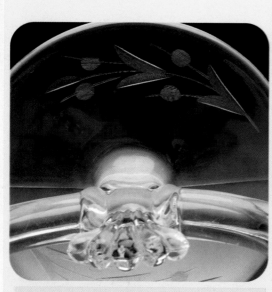

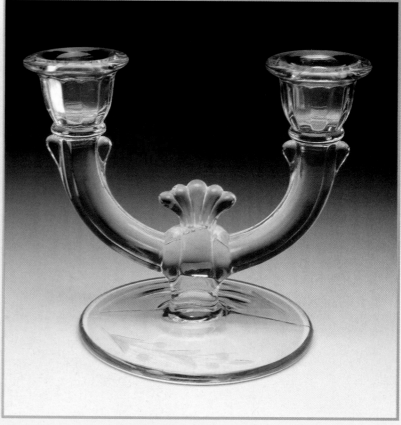

Company: **Paden City Glass**
Manufacturing Co.
Pattern: **Crow's Foot, #890 line, Floral**
Leaf cutting, 2-lite
Color: Crystal
Size: 5¼"
Value: $15.00

Company: **Paden City Glass Manufacturing Co.**
Pattern: **#2001, 2-lite**
Color: Crystal
Size: 4¼"
Value: $10.00

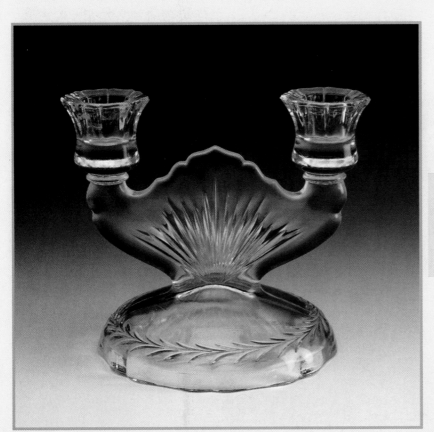

Company: **Jeannette Glass Co.**
Pattern: **Sunburst #1774**
Color: Crystal
Size: 5¼"
Value: $15.00

CRYSTAL

Company: **St. Clair Art Glass**
Pattern: **Handled Candleholder Paperweight**
Color: Crystal
Size: 3½"
Value: $40.00

Company: **L.E. Smith Glass Co.**
Pattern: **Swan Serenade #628**
Color: Crystal Satin
Size: 6"
Value: $14.00

Company: **L.E. Smith Glass Co.**
Pattern: **"Rose" #1951**
Color: Crystal (w/frost)
Size: 1½"
Value: $10.00

Company: **U.S. Glass Co./Tiffin**
Pattern: **"Web Wing" #5831, Flanders etch, 2-lite**
Color: Crystal
Size: 5¾"
Value: $45.00

Company: **L.E. Smith Glass Co.**
Pattern: **Pine Tree #6685**
Color: Crystal
Size: 9¼"
Value: $6.00

Company: **U.S. Glass Co./Tiffin**
Pattern: **Pearl Edge #5909,
                Tiffin Rose etch, 2-lite**
Color: Crystal
Size: 3" x 10"
Value: $45.00

CRYSTAL

Company: **U.S. Glass Co./Tiffin**
Pattern: **"Hercules," June Night etch**
Color: Crystal
Size: 4⅞"
Value: $50.00

Company: **U.S. Glass Co./Tiffin**
Pattern: **#5902, June Night etch, 2-lite, "Fan"**
Color: Crystal
Size: 5¾"
Value: $50.00

Company: **U.S. GlassCo./Tiffin**
Pattern: **Velva**
Color: Crystal
Size: 8¼"
Value: $80.00

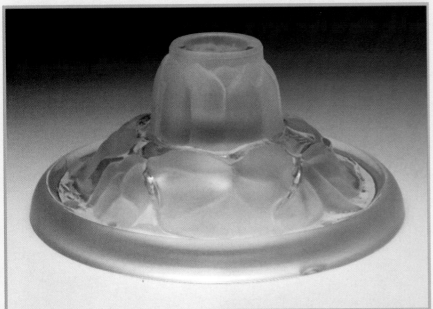

Company: **Verlys of France**
Pattern: **Water Lily**
Color: Crystal (satin)
Size: 2½"
Value: $20.00

Company: **Viking Glass Co.**
Pattern: **Epic #1196**
Color: Crystal
Size: 1¾"
Value: $6.00

CRYSTAL

Company: **Westmoreland Glass Co.**
Pattern: **Princess Feather #201, 2-lite**
Color: Crystal
Size: 5½"
Value: $35.00

Company: **Westmoreland Glass Co.**
Pattern: **Thousand Eye #1000**
Color: Crystal
Size: 5½"
Value: $25.00

Company: **Westmoreland Glass Co.**
Pattern: **Toy, 3-lite**
Color: Crystal
Size: 4½"
Value: $10.00

Company: **Westmoreland Glass Co.**
Pattern: **Mission #1015**
Color: Crystal
Size: 6¼"
Value: $30.00

Company: **Westmoreland Glass Co.**
Pattern: **Heart #1022**
Color: Crystal (w/silver overlay)
Size: 8"
Value: $40.00

CRYSTAL

Green

Company: **Anchor Hocking Glass Co.**
Pattern: **Oyster & Pearl #A881**
Color: Springtime Green
Size: 3¼"
Value: $12.00

Company: **Anchor Hocking Glass Co.**
Pattern: **Bubble**
Color: Forest Green
Size: 2"
Value: $125.00

Company: **Cambridge Glass Co.**
Pattern: **Star #3**
Color: Forest Green
Size: 5" wide
Value: $50.00

GREEN

136

Company: **Cambridge Glass Co.**
Pattern: **#227, etch #704**
Color: Light Emerald
Size: 1⅜"
Value: $20.00

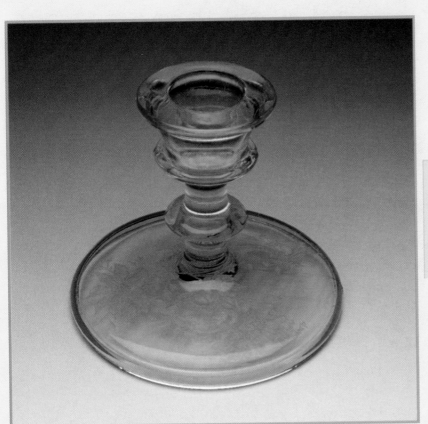

Company: **Cambridge Glass Co.**
Pattern: **#637, Early Wildflower
etch #517**
Color: Emerald
Size: 3½"
Value: $35.00

GREEN

Company: **Cambridge Glass Co.**
Pattern: **#638, Gloria etch #746,**
 Keyhole, 3-lite
Color: Green
Size: 6"
Value: $85.00

Company: **Cambridge Glass Co.**
Pattern: **Decagon #646,**
 Gloria etch #746
Color: Dark Emerald Green
Size: 5¾"
Value: $55.00

GREEN

Company: **Cambridge Glass Co.**
Pattern: **#647, 2-lite** (candelabrum)
Color: Dark Emerald
Size: 5½"
Value: $35.00

Company: **Cambridge Glass Co.**
Pattern: **Rosalie, etch #731** (above) **etch #703** (left)
Color: Emerald
Size: 4½"
Value: $35.00 ea.

GREEN

Company: **Dell Glass Co.**
Pattern: **Tulip**
Color: Green
Size: 3⅜"
Value: $35.00

Company: **Diamond Glass-ware Co.**
Pattern: **#625**
Color: Green
Size: 3¾"
Value: $15.00

Company: **Diamond Glass-ware Co.**
Pattern: **#713, crimped base**
Color: Green
Size: 2⅞"
Value: $15.00

Company: **Duncan and Miller Glass Co.**
Pattern: **#3, three-leaf**
Color: Green
Size: 2¾"
Value: $25.00

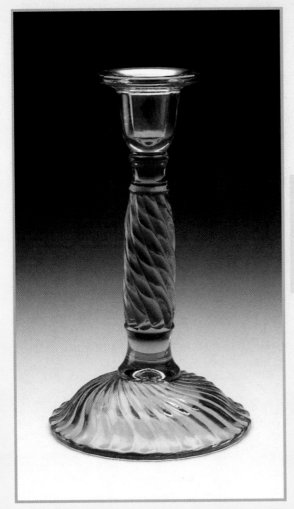

Company: **Duncan and Miller Glass Co.**
Pattern: **Spiral Flute #40**
Color: Green
Size: 9½"
Value: $60.00

Company: **Duncan and Miller Glass Co.**
Pattern: **Pharaoh**
Color: Green
Size: 2¾"
Value: $50.00

GREEN

Company: **Fenton Art Glass Co**.
Pattern: **#680**
Color: Emerald Crest/Milk
Size: 3¼"
Value: $37.50

Company: **Fenton Art Glass Co.**
Pattern: **Ruffled Hobnail #1932, 3-toe**
Color: Green
Size: 3" x 7½"
Value: $18.00

Company: **Fostoria Glass Co.**
Pattern: **#2297**
Color: Green
Size: 7"
Value: $30.00

GREEN

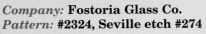

Company: **Fostoria Glass Co.**
Pattern: **#2324, Seville etch #274**
Color: Green
Size: 3"
Value: $20.00

Company: **Fostoria Glass Co.**
Pattern: **#2324 Brocade, Grape**
etch #287
Color: Green
Size: 3"
Value: $30.00

GREEN

Company: **Fostoria Glass Co.**
Pattern: **Spiral Optic #2372**
Color: Green
Size: 1½"
Value: $20.00

Company: **Fostoria Glass Co.**
Pattern: **#2455**
Color: Green
Size: 6"
Value: $50.00

Company: **Fostoria Glass Co.**
Pattern: **#2395 "Scroll," Oak Leaf etch #290**
Color: Green
Size: 3⅜"
Value: $45.00

Company: **Fostoria Glass Co.**
Pattern: **Heirloom #2726/311**
Color: Green Opalescent
Size: 3⅛"
Value: $30.00

Company: **Hazel-Atlas Glass Co.**
Pattern: **"Florentine" #2**
Color: Green
Size: 2½" x 4¼"
Value: $30.00

Company: **A.H. Heisey & Co.**
Pattern: **"Little Squatter" #99**
Color: Moongleam
Size: 1½"
Value: $25.00

GREEN

Company: **A.H. Heisey & Co.**
Pattern: **Mars #113**
Color: Moongleam (w/cut)
Size: 3½"
Value: $35.00

GREEN

Company: **Imperial Glass Co.**
Pattern: **Laced Edge #749**
Color: Seafoam Green
Size: 4½"
Value: $75.00

Company: **Imperial Glass Co.**
Pattern: **Heart #75, 3-lite**
Color: Stiegel Green
Size: 6⁹⁄₁₆"
Value: $50.00

Company: **Indiana Glass Co.**
Pattern: **#12**
Color: Green
Size: 4"
Value: $15.00

GREEN

Company: **Indiana Glass Co.**
Pattern: **Willow/Oleander #1008**
Color: Satinized Green, label reads
    "Desert Hue, California"
Size: 4¼"
Value: $35.00

Company: **Indiana Glass Co.**
Pattern: **Willow/Oleander #1008**
Color: Terrace Green
Size: 4"
Value: $45.00

Company: **Indiana Glass Co.**
Pattern: **Willow/Oleander #1008**
Color: Terrace Green
Size: 4⅛"
Value: $35.00

Company: **Indiana Glass Co.**
Pattern: **Unidentified, 2-lite**
Color: Terrace Green
Size: 5½"
Value: $30.00

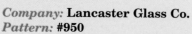

Company: **Lancaster Glass Co.**
Pattern: **#950**
Color: Applied Green over Crystal
Size: 7½"
Value: $25.00

Company: **Liberty Works**
Pattern: **Bamboo Optic**
Color: Green
Size: 3¼"
Value: $12.00

Company: **McKee Glass Co.**
Pattern: **Early American
        Rock Crystal**
Color: Green
Size: 2½"
Value: $40.00

Company: **New Martinsville Glass Co.**
Pattern: **Modernistic "Triad" #33**
Color: Jade Green (satin)
Size: 2½"
Value: $25.00

GREEN

Company: **New Martinsville Glass Co.**
Pattern: **Moondrops #37**
Color: Evergreen
Size: 2"
Value: $18.00

Company: **New Martinsville Glass Co.**
Pattern: **Moondrops #37/3**
Color: Evergreen
Size: 5"
Value: $65.00

Company: **Paden City Glass**
           Manufacturing Co.
Pattern: **Party Line #192**
Color: Green
Size: 3½"
Value: $15.00

GREEN

Company: **Paden City Glass Manufacturing Co.**
Pattern: **Crow's Foot "Mushroom" #412**
Color: Green
Size: 2¾"
Value: $35.00

Company: **Paden City Glass Manufacturing Co.**
Pattern: **"Triumph" #701**
Color: Green
Size: 2½"
Value: $18.00

Company: **Paden City Glass Manufacturing Co.**
Pattern: **Emerald Glo**
Color: Emerald
Size: 3¾"
Value: $17.50

GREEN

Company: **Paden City Glass
Manufacturing Co.**
Pattern: **Unidentified, cutting**
Color: Green
Size: 2⅞"
Value: $25.00

GREEN

Company: **L.E. Smith Glass Co.**
Pattern: **Mount Pleasant Double
Shield #600**
Color: Green
Size: 4½"
Value: $30.00

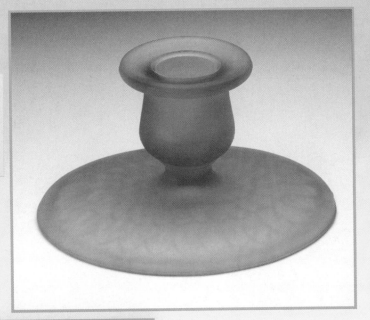

Company: **L.E. Smith Glass Co.**
Pattern: **"Feathers" #1400**
Color: Green satin
Size: 2⅜"
Value: $12.50

Company: **U.S. Glass Co./Tiffin**
Pattern: **#319**
Color: Green
Size: 2¾"
Value: $22.50

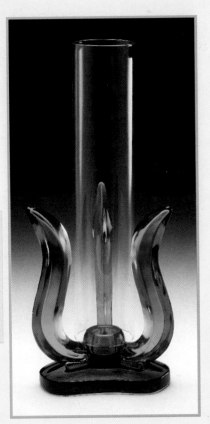

Company: **Viking Glass Co.**
Pattern: **Epic #1287** (hurricane candle w/shade)
Color: Emerald
Size: 6¾"
Value: $80.00 (set), $50.00 (candle), $30.00 (shade)

GREEN

Company: **Westmoreland Glass Co.**
Pattern: **Della Robbia #1058**
Color: Green Mist
Size: 3¼"
Value: $35.00

Company: **Westmoreland Glass Co.**
Pattern: **#1060**
Color: Green
Size: 5"
Value: $30.00

Company: **Westmoreland Glass Co.**
Pattern: **Lotus #1921** (twist stem)
Color: Green & Crystal
Size: 9"
Value: $75.00 (green), $50.00 (crystal)

Company: **Westmoreland Glass Co.**
Pattern: **Lotus #1921**
Color: Pink (left) 1960s; green (middle), 1920s;
        green (right) 1920s – 1960s
Size: 2¾" to 4"
Value: $20.00

GREEN

Company: **Westmoreland Glass Co.**
Pattern: **Spiral #1933**
Color: Mint Green Mist (left)
Mint Green (right)
Size: 6"
Value: $15.00

Modern Reproductions
Made in Taiwan

Multicolor

Company: Cambridge Glass Co.
Pattern: Dolphin #109
(Stratford)
Color: Crystal (w/flashing)
Size: 9½"
Value: $150.00

Company: Anchor Hocking Glass Co.
Pattern: Queen Mary #982
Color: Crystal (decorated w/red & yellow)
Size: 4"
Value: $35.00

Company: Cambridge Glass Co.
Pattern: Dolphin #109 (Stratford)
Color: Rubina
Size: 9½"
Value: $600.00

Company: Blenko Glass Co.
Pattern: Line #990A
Color: Yellow/Tangerine
Size: 2"
Value: $12.00

Company: **Indiana Glass Co.**
Pattern: **#301 Garland**
Color: Multicolored
Size: 5½"
Value: $35.00

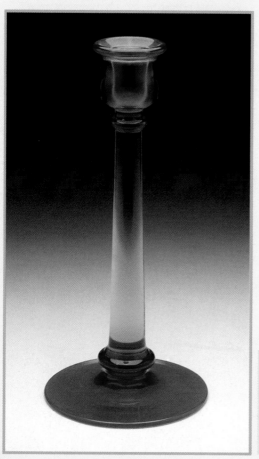

Company: **Indiana Glass Co.**
Pattern: **Wild Rose and Leaves**
Color: Marigold Carnival
Size: 2¼"
Value: $5.00

Company: **U.S. Glass Co./Tiffin**
Pattern: **#75**
Color: Amberina Red
Size: 9½"
Value: $65.00

Company: Anchor Hocking Glass Co.
Pattern: Block Optic
Color: Pink
Size: 1¾"
Value: $40.00

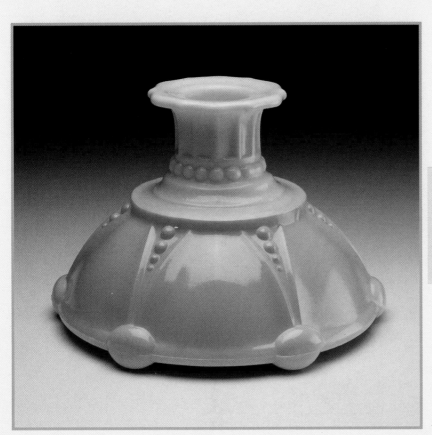

Company: Anchor Hocking Glass Co.
Pattern: Oyster & Pearl #881
("Dusty Rose")
Color: Pink/Vitrock
Size: 3¼"
Value: $12.50

Company: **Anchor Hocking Glass Co.**
Pattern: **Oyster & Pearl #A881**
Color: Pink
Size: 3¼"
Value: $15.00

Company: **Anchor Hocking Glass Co.**
Pattern: **Hurricane #1000**
Color: Flashed Pink
Size: 7" (w/shade)
Value: $15.00

Company: Beaumont Co.
Pattern: **Unidentified** (candleblock), **3-lite**
Color: Pink Frost (decorated)
Size: 3½"
Value: $85.00

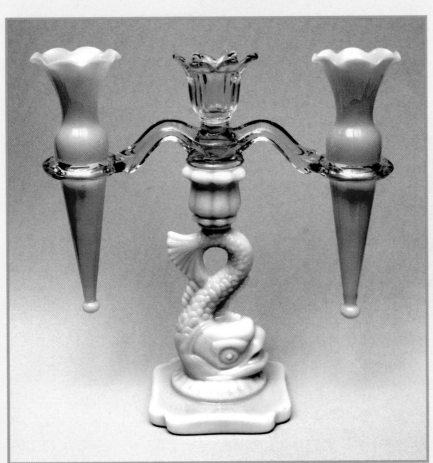

PINK

Company: Cambridge Glass Co.
Pattern: **Dolphin #50**
Color: Crown Tuscan
Size: 8"
Value: $650.00 (set),
$200.00 (candlestick),
$175.00 each (vases)
$100.00 #1438
(blue vase holder)

Company: **Cambridge Glass Co.**
Pattern: **Apple Blossom #627**
Color: Peach-blo
Size: 4"
Value: $35.00

Company: **Cambridge Glass Co.**
Pattern: **Decagon #647**
Color: Crown Tuscan (w/Gloria #746 decoration)
Size: 6"
Value: $150.00

Company: **Cambridge Glass Co.**
Pattern: **#647**
Color: Crown Tuscan (w/Rosepoint decoration)
Size: 6"
Value: $175.00

Company: **Cambridge Glass Co.**
Pattern: **#3011**
Color: Crown Tuscan (w/gold decoration)
Size: 9"
Value: $225.00 each

PINK

Company: **Cambridge Glass Co.**
Pattern: **Statuesque #3011**
Color: Crown Tuscan (w/gold silkscreen
  D-Lace 1007-8 decoration)
Size: 9"
Value: $1,250.00

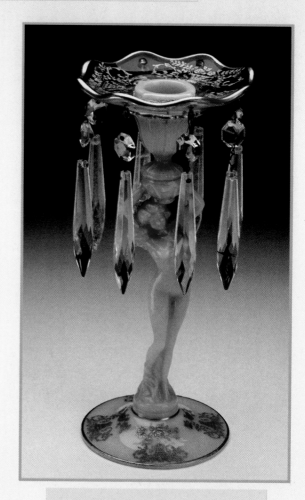

Company: **Cambridge Glass Co.**
Pattern: **Statuesque #3011**
Color: Crown Tuscan (w/gold Portia
  decoration)
Size: 8¾"
Value: $850.00

Company: **Cambridge Glass Co.**
Pattern: **Statuesque #3011**
Color: Crown Tuscan (w/gold Rosepoint
  decoration)
Size: 8¾"
Value: $1,250.00

PINK

Company: **Degenhart Co.**
Pattern: **Crystal Art Glass**
Color: Crown Tuscan
Size: 2¾"
Value: $50.00

Company: **Fenton Art Glass Co.**
Pattern: **#316**
Color: Persian Pearl/Pink Stretch
Size: 3½"
Value: $35.00

PINK

Company: **Fenton Art Glass Co.**
Pattern: **Ming, Cornucopia #950**
Color: Rose
Size: 5½"
Value: $30.00

PINK

Company: **Fostoria Glass Co.**
Pattern: **Heirloom #2183/311**
Color: Opalescent Pink
Size: 3"
Value: $50.00

Company: **Fostoria Glass Co.**
Pattern: **#2324, Grape Brocade etch #287**
Color: Orchid
Size: 3"
Value: $35.00

Company: **Fostoria Glass Co.**
Pattern: **Palm Leaf Brocade #2394**
Color: Rose (w/Mother of Pearl iridescence w/gold)
Size: 1¾" (candle), 12" (bowl)
Value: $35.00 (candle), $110.00 (bowl)

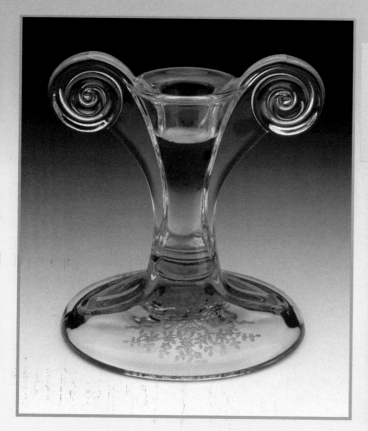

Company: **Fostoria Glass Co.**
Pattern: **Grecian #2395½,**
June etch
Color: Rose
Size: 5"
Value: $45.00

Company: **Fostoria Glass Co.**
Pattern: **Maypole #2412**
Color: Peach
Size: 9"
Value: $35.00

Company: **Fostoria Glass Co.**
Pattern: **#2415 Combination**
Bowl
Color: Rose
Size: 3½" x 12¾"
Value: $65.00

PINK

Company: **A.H. Heisey & Co.**
Pattern: **Raindrops #1205**
Color: Flamingo
Size: 1⅞"
Value: $45.00

Company: **A.H. Heisey & Co.**
Pattern: **Twist #1252**
Color: Pink
Size: 2"
Value: $35.00

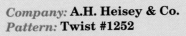

Company: **A.H. Heisey & Co.**
Pattern: **Sandwich #1404**
Color: Flamingo
Size: 6"
Value: $125.00

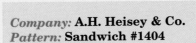

PINK

Company: **A.H. Heisey & Co.**
Pattern: **"Thumbprint & Panel"**
#1433, 2-lite
Color: Flamingo
Size: 5½"
Value: $65.00

Company: **Imperial Glass Co.**
Pattern: **#637**
Color: Pink (w/White Intaglio)
Size: 3⅜"
Value: $20.00

Company: **Indiana Glass Co.**
Pattern: **Tea Room #600**
Color: Pink
Size: 3"
Value: $40.00

Company: **Jeannette Glass Co.**
Pattern: **Adam**
Color: Pink
Size: 3¾"
Value: $50.00

PINK

Company: **Jeannette Glass Co.**
Pattern: **Holiday**
Color: Pink
Size: 3"
Value: $55.00

Company: **Jeannette Glass Co.**
Pattern: **Swirl**
Color: Pink
Size: 5½"
Value: $45.00

Company: **Lancaster Glass Co.**
Pattern: **Jungle Assortment #852**
Color: Rose Satin
Size: 1⅝"
Value: $25.00

Company: **McKee Glass Co.**
Pattern: **Optic #156, Brocade etch**
Color: Rose
Size: 2"
Value: $25.00

PINK

Company: **McKee Glass Co.**
Pattern: **Optic #156**
Color: Rose
Size: 2"
Value: $15.00

Company: **McKee Glass Co.**
Pattern: **Brocade #200**
      (w/octagonal base)
Color: Rose
Size: 2⅞"
Value: $20.00

Company: **Morgantown Glass Works**
    (undocumented but accepted
    by Morgantown collectors)
Pattern: **Unidentified**
Color: Pink
Size: 4"
Value: $30.00

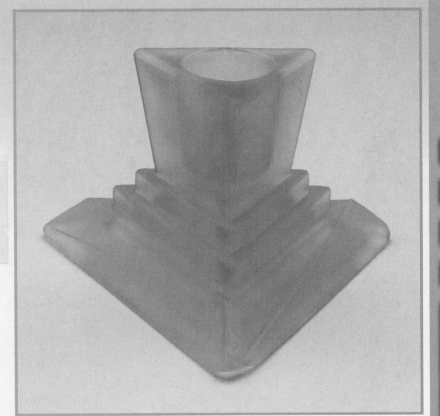

Company: **New Martinsville Glass Co.**
Pattern: **Modernistic "Triad" #33**
Color: Pink (satin)
Size: 2½"
Value: $30.00

Company: **Paden City Glass
Manufacturing Co.**
Pattern: **Party Line #191, skirted**
Color: Cheriglo (w/decoration)
Size: 4⅛"
Value: $15.00

PINK

177

Company: **Paden City Glass Manufacturing Co.**
Pattern: **Archaic #300, Cupid etch**
Color: Cheriglo
Size: 1⅞"
Value: $100.00

Company: **Paden City Glass Manufacturing Co.**
Pattern: **Regina Blank #210, Black Forest**
Color: Cheriglo
Size: 2¾"
Value: $50.00

Company: **Paden City Glass Manufacturing Co.**
Pattern: **Crow's Foot #412**
Color: Cheriglo
Size: 5⅜"
Value: $25.00

PINK

Company: **L.E. Smith Glass Co.**
Pattern: **"Feathers" #1400** (Swan set)
Color: Pink Satin
Size: 2⅜" (candles)
Value: $95.00 (set) – $35.00 (swan), $20.00 (frog), $20.00 each (candlesticks)

Company: **U.S. Glass Co./Tiffin**
Pattern: **Deerwood #101**
Color: Rose
Size: 2½"
Value: $50.00

Company: **U.S. Glass Co./Tiffin**
Pattern: **Sylvan #101, Rose etch**
Color: Rose
Size: 2½"
Value: $40.00

PINK

Company: **Westmoreland Glass Co.**
Pattern: **Lotus #1921**
Color: Pink (satin)
Size: 5¼"
Value: $35.00

Company: **U.S. Glass Co.**
Pattern: **Puritan**
Color: Pink (matte finish w/decoration)
Size: 9⅛"
Value: $40.00

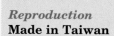

Reproduction
Made in Taiwan

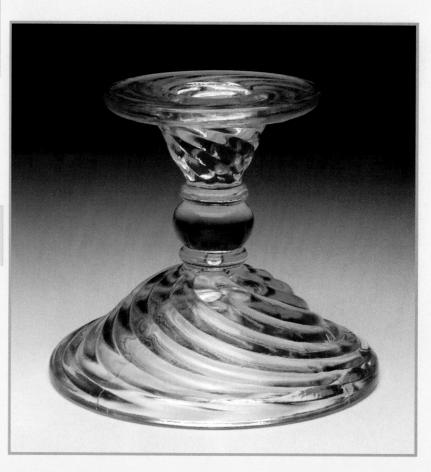

PINK

Purple

Company: **Paden City Glass
              Manufacturing Co.**
Pattern: **"Bird on a Perch" #115**
Color: Purple
Size: 9"
Value: $75.00

Company: **Westmoreland Glass Co.**
Pattern: **Lotus #1921**
Color: Lilac (cased)
Size: 3⅞"
Value: $35.00

Company: **Westmoreland Glass Co.**
Pattern: **Lotus #1921** (twist stem)
Color: Lilac (cased)
Size: 9"
Value: $75.00

Company: **Westmoreland Glass Co.**
Pattern: **"Doric Column" #1002**
Color: Purple (painted)
Size: 8"
Value: $30.00

Red

Company: **Anchor Hocking Glass Co.**
Pattern: **Early American Prescut #784**
Color: Sprayed Red
Size: 5⅝"
Value: $35.00

Company: **Anchor Hocking Glass Co.**
Pattern: **Queen Mary #982**
Color: Royal Ruby
Size: 4"
Value: $100.00

Company: **Cambridge Glass Co.**
Pattern: **Dolphin #50** (Seashell line)
Color: Carmen
Size: 8"
Value: $400.00

Company: **Cambridge Glass Co.**
Pattern: **Tally Ho #1402/76**
Color: Carmen
Size: 5"
Value: $55.00

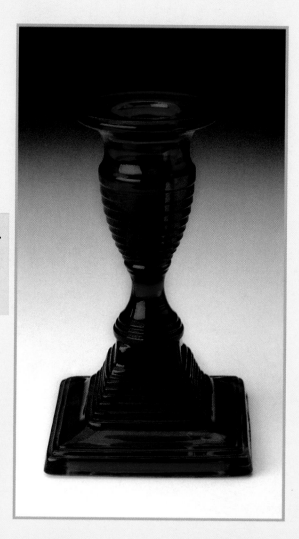

Company: **Cambridge Glass Co.**
Pattern: **Tally Ho #1402/80**
Color: Carmen
Size: 6½"
Value: $100.00

Company: **Cambridge Glass Co.**
Pattern: **Tally Ho #1402/80**
Color: Carmen (w/gold silkscreen D-Lace 1007-8)
Size: 6½"
Value: $400.00

RED

Company: **Cambridge Glass Co.**
Pattern: **#1192**
Color: Carmen (w/sterling overlay)
Size: 6"
Value: $250.00

Company: **Cambridge Glass Co.**
Pattern: **Sonata #1957/121**
Color: Carmen
Size: 5⅜"
Value: $45.00

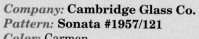

Company: **Fostoria Glass Co.**
Pattern: **Luxembourg #2766/311**
                (crown trindle bowl)
Color: Red
Size: 4¾"
Value: $75.00

Company: **Imperial Glass Co.**
Pattern: **Olive #134**
Color: Ruby
Size: 2½"
Value: $15.00

Company: **Indiana Glass Co.**
Pattern: **"Block & Rib" #370**
Color: Red Stain (w/Orchid)
Size: 5¼"
Value: $25.00

RED

Company: Indiana Glass Co.
Pattern: Diamond Point (made from
shakers w/metal insert
for candle)
Color: Red (flashed)
Size: 3"
Value: $9.00 each

RED

Company: Morgantown Glass Works
Pattern: Golf Ball #7643 (Jacobi)
Color: Spanish Red
Size: 4"
Value: $110.00

Company: **Morgantown Glass Works**
Pattern: **Golf Ball #7643 (DuPont)**
Color: Spanish Red
Size: 4"
Value: $150.00

Company: **Morgantown Glass Works**
Pattern: **Old Bristol #1**
Color: Spanish Red (w/alabaster-white stem)
Size: 3⅝"
Value: $400.00

RED

Company: **New Martinsville Glass Co.**
Pattern: **Moondrops #37**
(Ruffled Sherbet style)
Color: Ruby
Size: 2⅝"
Value: $30.00

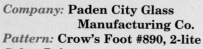

Company: **Paden City Glass Manufacturing Co.**
Pattern: **Crow's Foot #890, 2-lite**
Color: Ruby
Size: 5¼"
Value: $50.00

Company: **New Martinsville Glass Co.**
Pattern: **Moondrops #37/2 ("Wings")**
Color: Ruby
Size: 5"
Value: $40.00

Company: Paden City Glass
                    Manufacturing Co.
Pattern: **Nerva**
Color: Ruby
Size: 5¾"
Value: $50.00

Company: **L.E. Smith Glass Co.**
Pattern: **Wig-Wam**
Color: Red
Size: 3"
Value: $25.00

RED

Company: U.S. Glass Co./Tiffin
Pattern: King's Crown #4016-18,
2-lite
Color: Red/Crystal, Cranberry Flash
Size: 5½"
Value: $85.00

Company: Westmoreland Glass Co.
Pattern: English Hobnail #555
Color: Ruby
Size: 8"
Value: $50.00

Company: Westmoreland Glass Co.
Pattern: Paneled Grape #1881
Color: Crystal (w/Ruby stain)
Size: 4"
Value: $15.00

Company: **Westmoreland Glass Co.**
Pattern: **Lotus #1921**
Color: Crystal (w/Ruby stain)
Size: 3¾"
Value: $15.00

Company: **Westmoreland Glass Co.**
Pattern: **Wakefield #1932**
Color: Red Crystal (w/Ruby stain)
Size: 6"
Value: $47.50

RED

Company: **Westmoreland Glass Co.**
Pattern: **Wakefield Fairy Lamps** (piece on left is top shade for base in center)
Color: Ruby (right), Ruby Crystal (center)
Size: 6"
Value: $95.00 (Ruby), $70.00 (Ruby Crystal)

Company: **Westmoreland Glass Co.**
Pattern: **Ball & Swirl #1842**
Color: Ruby (stained)
Size: 3¾"
Value: $20.00

Company: *Cambridge Glass Co.*
Pattern: **Caprice #72, 2-lite**
Color: Smoke
Size: 6"
Value: $250.00

Company: **Consolidated Lamp &**
Glass Co.
Pattern: **Martelé Vine #708**
Color: Sepia Wash
Size: 3¾"
Value: $50.00

Company: **Consolidated Lamp &**
Glass Co.
Pattern: **Ruba Rhombic #805**
Color: Smoky Topaz
Size: 2½"
Value: $175.00

Company: **Cambridge Glass Co.**
Pattern: **Mt. Vernon #110**
Color: Milk
Size: 5"
Value: $75.00

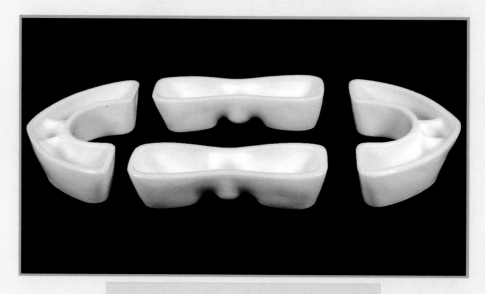

Company: **Fenton Art Glass Co.**
Pattern: **Clusterette #1952/9002** (flower set)
Color: Milk
Size: 1⅝"
Value: $60.00 set

WHITE

Company: **Fenton Art Glass Co.**
Pattern: **Hobnail #3672, 2-lite**
Color: Milk
Size: 5½"
Value: $60.00

Company: **Fenton Art Glass Co.**
Pattern: **Hobnail #3674**
Color: Milk
Size: 5⅞"
Value: $25.00

WHITE

Company: **Fenton Art Glass Co.**
Pattern: **Hobnail #3745** (candleholder
            base), **#3742** (low bowl), **2-pc. set**
Color: Milk
Size: 7" (candlestick only), 9⅛" (w/bowl)
Value: $28.00 (candlesticks only),
            $55.00 (bowl), $83.00 (set)

Company: **Fenton Art Glass Co.**
Pattern: **Hobnail #3870**
Color: Milk
Size: 3¼"
Value: $25.00

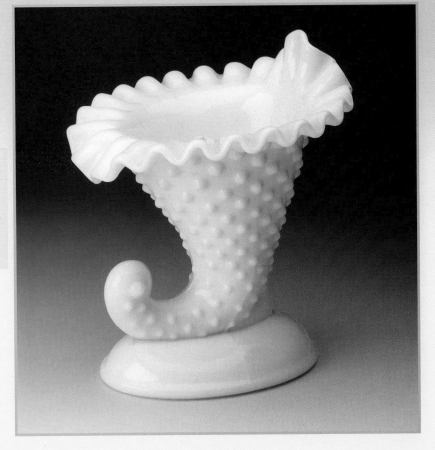

Company: **Fenton Art Glass Co.**
Pattern: **Hobnail, Cornucopia**
#3874
Color: Milk
Size: 6⅛"
Value: $30.00

Company: **Fenton Art Glass Co.**
Pattern: **Hobnail #3974**
Color: Milk
Size: 3¼"
Value: $12.00

WHITE

Company: **Fenton Art Glass Co.**
Pattern: **Hobnail #3998**
Color: Milk
Size: 8¼"
Value: $50.00

Company: **Fenton Art Glass Co.**
(for Tiara Exclusives)
Pattern: **Water Lily #8473** (or #611
in old catalog reprint)
Color: White Satin
Size: 3"
Value: $15.00

Company: **Imperial Glass Co.**
Pattern: **#280**
Color: Milk
Size: 4"
Value: $15.00

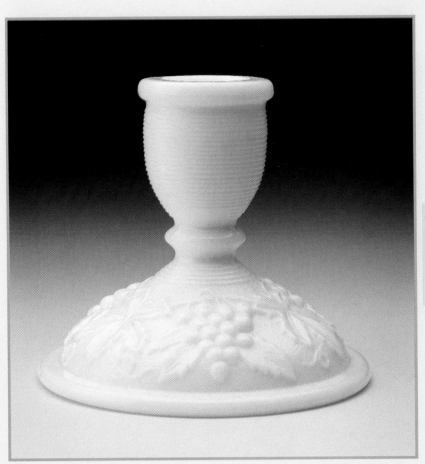

Company: **Imperial Glass Co.**
Pattern: **Grape #1950/880**
Color: Milk
Size: 3⅜"
Value: $10.00

Company: **Indiana Glass Co.**
Pattern: **Harvest #2970**
Color: Milk
Size: 4"
Value: $8.00

Company: **McKee Glass Co.**
Pattern: **Early American**
              Rock Crystal
              (Double candle)
Color: Milk
Size: 4⅛"
Value: $18.00

Company: **Phoenix Glass Co.**
Pattern: **Sawtooth**
Color: Milk (w/Antique Blue decoration)
Size: 6¾"
Value: $35.00

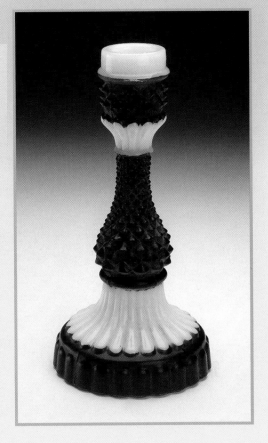

Company: **L.E. Smith Glass Co.**
Pattern: **#408**
Color: Milk
Size: 3¼"
Value: $10.00

Company: **Westmoreland Glass Co.**
Pattern: **Ring & Petal #1875**
Color: Milk
Size: 3½"
Value: $12.50

WHITE

Company: **Westmoreland Glass Co.**
Pattern: **Lotus #1921**
Color: Milk
Size: 5¼"
Value: $25.00

Company: **Westmoreland Glass Co.**
Pattern: **Spiral #1933**
Color: Milk
Size: 6½"
Value: $10.00

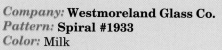

Yellow

Company: **Cambridge Glass Co.**
Pattern: **Dolphin #109**
Color: Ivory (Custard)
Size: 9½"
Value: $350.00

Company: **Cambridge Glass Co.**
Pattern: **#636, Apple Blossom etch #744**
Color: Gold Krystol
Size: 9½"
Value: $100.00

Company: **Cambridge Glass Co.**
Pattern: **#638, Gloria etch #746,
3-lite**
Color: Gold Krystol (gold encrusted)
Size: 6"
Value: $85.00

Company: **Fostoria Glass Co.**
Pattern: **Versailles #2375,
etch #278**
Color: Topaz
Size: 3¼"
Value: $30.00

Company: **Fostoria Glass Co.**
Pattern: **Three-toe #2394,**
            June etch #279
Color: Topaz
Size: 2"
Value: $30.00

YELLOW

Company: **Fostoria Glass Co.**
Pattern: **Three-toe #2394, New**
            Garland etch #284
Color: Topaz
Size: 2"
Value: $25.00

Company: **Fostoria Glass Co.**
Pattern: **Maypole #2412/314**
Color: Yellow
Size: 3¼"
Value: $25.00

Company: **Fostoria Glass Co.**
Pattern: **"Twenty Four Seventy"**
#2470, Legion etch #309
Color: Topaz
Size: 5¾"
Value: $60.00

Company: **Fostoria Glass Co.**
Pattern: **Baroque #2496**
        (Sakier design)
Color: Gold Tint
Size: 5¾"
Value: $35.00

Company: **Fostoria Glass Co.**
Pattern: **Baroque Trindle #2496**
Color: Gold Tint
Size: 5⅝"
Value: $50.00

YELLOW

Company: Fostoria Glass Co.
Pattern: Heirloom #2772/312 (peg vase);
#2772/460 (candle/ snack bowl);
#2772/334 (trindle candle)
Color: Yellow Opalescent (arm of trindle candle, crystal)
Size: Peg vase, 7⅞"; candle/snack bowl, 3" x 5"; trindle candle, 2¼" x 7½"
Value: Peg vase, $40.00; candle/snack bowl, $30.00 each; trindle candle, $20.00

Company: Fostoria Glass Co.
Pattern: Heirloom #1515/311 (candlevase)
Color: Yellow Opalescent
Size: 8½"
Value: $60.00

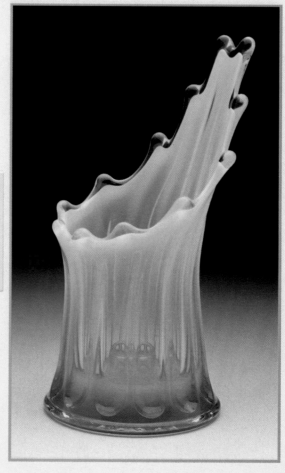

Company: **A.H. Heisey & Co.**
Pattern: **"Trident" #134, 2-lite**
Color: Sahara
Size: 6"
Value: $65.00

Company: **A.H. Heisey & Co.**
Pattern: **Old Sandwich #1404**
Color: Sahara
Size: 6"
Value: $95.00

YELLOW

Company: **A.H. Heisey & Co.**
Pattern: **Thumbprint and Panel #1433**
Color: Sahara
Size: 5½"
Value: $65.00

Company: **A.H. Heisey & Co.**
Pattern: **Ridgeleigh #1469**
Color: Sahara
Size: 4½"
Value: $75.00

Company: **Indiana Glass Co.**
Pattern: **Moderne Classic #603**
Color: Yellow (w/applied decoration)
Size: 3¾"
Value: $25.00

Company: **Indiana Glass Co.**
Pattern: **Celestial #12011**
Color: Yellow Mist
Size: 1¼"
Value: $5.00

Company: **Lancaster Glass Co.**
Pattern: **"Jodi" #355/3**
Color: Topaz
Size: 2⅝"
Value: $12.50

Company: **Lancaster Glass Co.**
Pattern: **#86/950**
Color: Yellow (sprayed)
Size: 7½"
Value: $20.00

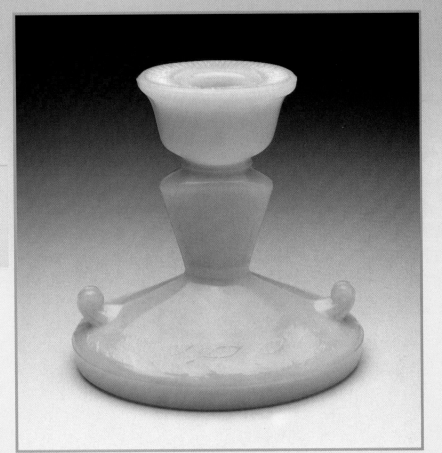

Company: **McKee Glass Co.**
Pattern: **Laurel**
Color: French Ivory
Size: 4"
Value: $30.00

Company: **U.S. Glass Co./Tiffin**
Pattern: **La Fleur #101**
Color: Mandarin
Size: 2½"
Value: $35.00

YELLOW

Company: **U.S. Glass Co.**
Pattern: **#319**
Color: Canary (satin)
Size: 8"
Value: $45.00

Company: **U.S. Glass Co./Tiffin**
Pattern: **Byzantine #5831**
Color: Mandarin
Size: 3¾"
Value: $35.00

YELLOW

Company: **Westmoreland Glass Co.**
Pattern: **Lotus #1921** (twist stem)
Color: Cased Yellow
Size: 9"
Value: $75.00

Company: **Anchor Hocking Glass Co.**
Pattern: **Oyster & Pearl #A881**
Color: Vitrock
Size: 3¼"
Value: $10.00

YELLOW

Anchor Hocking Glass Co.
#982 63
Block Optic 161
Bubble 62, 136
Early American Prescut #784 . .183
Hurricane #1000 162
Oyster & Pearl #881
   ("Dusty Rose") 161
Oyster & Pearl #A881 .136, 162, 217
Queen Mary #982 . . .62, 159, 183
Wexford 63
Beaumont Co.
Triple Candle 64
Unidentified (candleblock) . . .163
Blenko Glass Co.
Line #9516 65
Line #990A 64, 159
Bryce Brothers Co.
Aquarius 6
Cambridge Glass Co.
#68 24
#227 137
#227½ 67
#437 24
#437 38
#627 69
#636 205
#637 137
#638 138
#638 206
#647 (Heatherbloom) 16
#647, Elaine 70
#647 (Dark Emerald) 139
#647, Rosepoint (gold) 165
#1192 186
#1273 39
#1355 & 1356 40
#1442 40
#1545 41
#1604 Chantilly 77
#2798 17
#3011 165
#3121 Wildflower 79
#3900/67 79
Apple Blossom #627 164
Candelabrum parts 81
Caprice #72 195
Caprice #74 66
Caprice #1357 75
Cascade #4000/67 80
Cherub #1191 . . . . .25, 72
Corinth #3900/68 80
Cut Harvest #1613 78
Decagon #646 39
Decagon #646, Apple Blossom .15
Decagon #646, Gloria 138
Decagon #647 164
Decagon #878 (Charleton
   decoration) 16
Decagon #878, Majestic 71

Diane #646 38
"Dolphin" (Fish) #67 66
Dolphin #109 (aka Stratford) . .205
Dolphin #109 (aka Stratford),
   Crystal 159
Dolphin #109 (aka Stratford),
   Rubina 159
Dolphin #50 (Crystal) 65
Dolphin #50 (Crown Tuscan) . .163
Dolphin #50 (Seashell line) . . .184
Dolphin #612 (clear) 78
Dolphin #612 (w/gold) 78
Doric Column #65 37
Epergnette #1580 77
Everglade #1155 72
Flower Frog #1504 76
Flower Frog #1505 76
Gadroon #3500/32 6
Gadroon #3500/108 79
Imperial Hunt Scene #638 24
Martha #495 67
Moderne 41
Mt. Vernon #38 15
Mt. Vernon #110 196
Pristine #500 68
Pristine #510 69
"Ram's Head/Cornucopia"
   #657 71
Rosalie, #731 139
Roselyn, #646 "Keyhole" 70
Rosepoint #1338 (plain) 74
Rosepoint #1338 (w/gold) 75
Rosepoint Candelabrum parts .81
Sonata #1957/121 186
Square #3797/67 6
Star 37
Star #3 136
Statuesque #3011 42
Statuesque #3011
   (w/gold Portia) 166
Statuesque #3011
   (w/gold Rosepoint) 166
Statuesque #3011
   (w/gold silkscreen) 166
Tally Ho #1402/76 184
Tally Ho #1402/80 76
Tally Ho #1402/80 (plain) 185
Tally Ho #1402/80
   (w/gold silkscreen) 185
Triple Candle #1307 73
Triple Candle #1307, Chintz . . .73
Triple Candle #1307, Marjorie . .74
Tulip #1438 17
Unidentified 42
Virginian #502 68
Central Glass Works
#2000 43
Chippendale 82
Harding #2000 18
Spiral #1426 7

Unidentified 7
Colony Glassware
Whitehall 82
Consolidated Lamp & Glass Co.
Catalonian (Old Spanish) 18
Martelé Vine #708 195
Ruba Rhombic #805 195
Dalzell Viking
Flame, "Squirrel" #8566 25
Princess Plaza #5515 25
Degenhart Co.
Crystal Art Glass 167
Dell Glass Co.
Tulip 140
Tulip (candlebowl) 19
Tulip (candlestick) 19
Diamond Glass-ware Co.
#99 26
#625 . . . . .27, 140
#713 140
Gothic #716 27
Trumpet Shape 28
Duncan and Miller Glass Co.
#3 141
#4 .83
#16 28
#50 43
#65 84
Canterbury Line #115 . . . .85, 86
Early American Sandwich
   #41-125 84
Festive #155/60 44
First Love #1-4 83
Pharaoh 141
Puritan 87
Quilted Diamond #44 8
Ripple #101 8
Spiral Flute #40 141
Teardrop #301 87
Terrace #111 44
Terrace #111, First Love 85
"Three Feathers" #117 44
Tropical Fish 88
"Venetian" #5 43
**Duncan and Miller Glass Co.,
U.S. Glass Co./Tiffin**
Murano #125 86
Federal Glass Co.
#2758 Petal 88
Pioneer #2806 1/2 88
Fenton Art Glass Co.
#314 45
#316 167
#680 142
#848 45
#2318 28

Clusterette #1952/9002
   (Flower set) 196
Hobnail #3672 197

Hobnail #3674 197
Hobnail #3742 198
Hobnail #3745 198
Hobnail #3870 198
Hobnail #3974 199
Hobnail #3998 200
Hobnail, Cornucopia #3874 . .199
Ming, Cornucopia #950 168
Ruffled Hobnail #1932 142
Silvertone #1011 9
Water Lily #8473 200

Fostoria Glass Co.
#2297 142
#2324 Brocade 143
#2324 Columbine Variant Cut . .48
#2324, Grape Brocade 169
#2324, Mt. Vernon 20
#2324, Seville 143
#2324 (w/gold decoration) 49
#2324 (w/silver overlay) 89
#2375 .49
#2393 .20
#2395 "Scroll" 144
#2415 Combination Bowl 170
#2455 144
#2484 Trindle 91
#2485 .47
#2535 .94
#2639 Duo 98
#2668/459 99
Baroque #2496 47
Baroque #2496, Corsage 92
Baroque #2496, Navarre 92
Baroque #2496 (Sakier design) 209
Baroque Trindle #2496 209
Century #2630 97
Century Duo #2630 97
Colony Glassware #2412 90
Coronation 89
Coronet #2560 95
Coronet #2560½ 95
Duo-Candle Blank #2472 91
Fairfax #2375, Acanthus 10
Fairfax #2375 (w/silver
    decorations) 49
Fairfax #2375, June 90
Fairfax #2375½ 50
Fairfax #2375½ (clear) 46
Fairfax #2375½, Versailles 46
Flame Duo #2545 48
Garden Center #2640 99
Glacier #2510 93
Grecian #2395½ 170
Heirloom #1515/311 (Blue
    Opalescent) 46
Heirloom #1515/311 (Yellow
    Opalescent) 210
Heirloom #2183/311 168
Heirloom #2726/311 145
Heirloom #2772/312 210
Heirloom #2772/334 210
Heirloom #2772/460 210
Lily #2352 9
Luxembourg #2766/311 186
Maypole #2412 170
Maypole #2412/314 208

Myraid #2592 95
"Nocturne" #2527 94
Palm Leaf Brocade #2324 169
Plume #2594 96
Plume #2636 98
Quadrangle #2546 94
Scroll #2395 29
Scroll #2395½ 30
Sonata Duo #6023 100
Spiral Optic #2372 144
Sunray #2510 93
Three-toe #2394, June #279 . . .207
Three-toe #2394, New Garland
    #284 207
Trindle #2383 29
"Twenty Four Seventy" #2470 .208
Versailles #2375 206
Wistar #2620 96

H.C. Fry Glass Co.
Unidentified (Amber) 10
Unidentified (Ebony) 30

Hazel-Atlas Glass Co.
"Florentine" #2 145
Royal Lace 100
Royal Lace Ruffled 50
Star #930 21

A. H. Heisey & Co.
#4233 (peg vase) 109
Block Five #1619 109
Cabochon #1951 110
Cascade #142 101
Crystolite #1502 103
Crystolite #1503 (2-lite) 104
Crystolite #1503 (w/block) 103
Crystolite #1503 (w/o block) . .104
Crystolite #1503¼ 104
Empire #1471 102
Fern #1495 103
"Fish" #1550 108
Flame #1615 109
Four Leaf #1552 108
Lariat #1540 (2-lite) 106
Lariat #1540 (3-lite) 107
Lariat #1540
    (black-out lamp) 106
Lariat #1540, Moonglo 107
"Little Squatter" #99 145
Mars #113 146
Mercury #112 101
Old Sandwich #1404 . . . . .51, 211
Plantation #1567 (hurricane) . .108
Raindrops #1205 171
Ridgeleigh #1469 212
Ridgeleigh #1496½ 102
Sandwich #1404 171
Skirted Panel #33 101
Thumbprint and Panel #1433 . .212
"Trident" #134 211
"Trident" #134, Narcissus 110
"Trident" #134, Orchid 111
"Trident" #134,
    Rose of Peace 111
Twist #1252 171
Victorian #1425 102
Waverly #1519, Orchid 105
Waverly #1519, Rose 106

Whirlpool #1506
    (aka "Provincial") 105
Imperial Glass Co.
#148 112
#280 201
#607 114
#637 172
#782 115
Candlewick #400/66F 113
Candlewick #400/86 51
Candlewick Twin #400/100 . . .113
Cathay #5009 116
Cathay Candle Servant
    #5033 (man) 117
Cathay Candle Servant
    #5034 (woman) 117
Cathay Pillow #5013 116
Cathay Shen #5020/2 116
Cathay Wedding Lamp
    #5027 117
Corinthian #280/100 112
"Double Heart" #753 115
Empire Dolphin #779 52
Flute 'N Cane
    (aka Amelia) 114
Grape #1950/880 201
Heart #75 147
Laced Edge #749 146
Olive #134 (Ruby) 187
Olive #134 (Viennese Blue) . . .51
Reeded/"Spun" #701 114
Twin #153 11
Indiana Glass Co.
#12 .147
#301 Garland 160
#303 118
#603 .52
#1006 119
"Block & Rib" #370 (Crystal) . .118
"Block & Rib" #370
    (Red Stain w/Orchid) 187
"Block & Rib" (candlesticks) .122
"Block & Rib" (footed bowl) .122
Celestial #12011 213
Diamond Point 188
Harvest #2970 202
Laurel #1010 121
Laurel #1010 (2-lite) 122
Moderne Classic #603 213
Tea Room #600 (Crystal) 119
Tea Room #600 (Pink) 173
Unidentified (2-lite) 149
Wedgewood #4 52
Wild Rose and Leaves 160
Willow/Oleander #1007
    (2-lite, gold) 119
Willow/Oleander #1007
    (2-lite, satin) 120
Willow/Oleander #1008
    (2-lite) 53
Willow/Oleander #1008
    (bowl) 120
Willow/Oleander #1008
    (candlebowl) 148
Willow/Oleander #1008
    (candlestick) 121, 148, 149

Indiana Glass Co. for Colony Glassware
Epergne 123
Jeannette Glass Co.
Adam 173
Holiday 174
Sunburst #1774 129
Swirl 174
Lancaster Glass Co.
#86/950 214
#950 150
Deco Style 123
"Jodi" #355/3 214
Jungle Assortment #852 175
Libbey Glass Co.
Worthington #4084 26
Liberty Works
Bamboo Optic 150
McKee Glass Co.
Autumn 53
Brocade #200 176
Early American Rock Crystal .150, 202
Laurel 215
Optic #156 (clear) 175
Optic #156, Brocade 175
Scalloped Edge #157 31
Modern Reproductions
Made in Taiwan 158, 180
Morgantown Glass Works
"Blinken" 31
Classic #88 54
Federal #9935 54
Golf Ball #7643 54
Golf Ball #7643 (DuPont) 189
Golf Ball #7643 (Jacobi) 188
Majesty #7662 . . . . .21, 55
Old Bristol #1 189
"Royal #1304 31
"Winken" 31
Unidentified 176
Morgantown Guild
Moonscape #3045 32
New Martinsville Glass Co.
#10 .32
#453 11
#652 Cornucopia 124
#671 Shell 124
"Addie" #18 33
Janice #4585 56
Modernistic "Triad" #33 . .151, 177
Moondrops #37 (candle) 22
Moondrops #37 (candlebowl) .151
Moondrops #37 (Ruffled) 190
Moondrops #37/2
  ("Wings," Amber) 12
Moondrops #37/2 ("Wings,"
  Ruby) 190
Moondrops #37/3 152
Radiance #42 (Amber) 12
Radiance #42 (Colonial Blue) .55
Scroll #1076 124

Swan Line #451 123
Teardrop #4457 125
Paden City Glass Manufacturing Co.
#215 (Glades line) 126
#220 (Largo line, clear) 125
#220 (Largo line, w/silver
  overlay) 126
#300 Archaic 57
#555 line, Floral 128
#555 line (plain) 127
#2001 129
Archaic #300 178
"Bird on a Perch" #115 181
Crow's Foot "Mushroom" #412 .153
Crow's Foot #412, Ardith 33
Crow's Foot #412 (clear) 178
Crow's Foot #890 190
Crow's Foot #890 line 128
Crow's Foot Round #890 13
Emerald Glo 153
Largo #220 56
Nerva 191
Party Line #191 12
Party Line #191 (skirted) 177
Party Line #192 152
Regina Blank #210 178
"Sasha Bird"/Crow's Foot #412 .127
"Triumph" #701 153
Unidentified 154
Pairpoint Corporation
"Grape" Etched 22
Phoenix Glass Co.
Sawtooth 203
Sinclaire & Co.
#12928 58
L. E. Smith Glass Co.
"Feathers" #1400 155
"Feathers" #1400 (Swan set) . .179
#408 203
Loop Handle #408 34
Mt. Pleasant Double Shield
  #600 154
Mt. Pleasant Double Shield
  #600/4 57
Mt. Pleasant Double Shield
  (candlebowl) 35
Mt. Pleasant Double Shield
  (candlestick) 34
Pine Tree #6685 131
"Rose" #1951 130
Swan Serenade #628 130
Wig-Wam 191
St. Clair Art Glass
Handled Candleholder
  Paperweight 130
U. S. Glass Co.
#18 .23
#76 .58
#94 .59
#300 59
#319 216

Hobnail #518 23
Puritan 180
Ribbed #18 35
U. S. Glass Co./Tiffin
#75 160
#319 155
#5902 132
#6125 60
Brocade #326 13
Byzantine #5831 216
Deerwood #101 . . . . .36, 179
"Hercules" 132
King's Crown #4016-18 192
La Fleur #101 215
Pearl Edge #5909 131
Sylvan #101 179
Twisted 60
Velva 133
"Web Wing" #5831 131
Utility Glass Works
Cambodian Line 22
Verlys of France
Water Lily 133
Viking Glass Co.
Astra/Epic #6112 61
Epic #1196 (Blunique) 61
Epic #1196 (Crystal) 133
Epic #1287 155
Epic #1409 23
Westmoreland Glass Co.
#1060 156
Ball & Swirl #1842 194
Della Robbia #1058 156
"Doric Column #1002 182
English Hobnail #555 14
English Hobnail #555 192
Heart #1022 135
Lotus #1921 (candlebowl) 14
Lotus #1921 (candles) 157
Lotus #1921 (twist stem, Green &
  Crystal)) 157
Lotus #1921 (3-lite, Pink) 180
Lotus #1921 (Lilac) 181
Lotus #1921 (Crystal w/Ruby
  stain) 193
Lotus #1921 (3-lite, Milk) 204
Lotus #1921 (twist stem,
  Cased Yellow) 217
Lotus #1921 (twist stem, Lilac) .182
Mission #1015 135
Octagon Candle #1211-2 36
Paneled Grape #1881 192
Princess Feather #201 134
Ring & Petal #1875 203
Spiral #1933 (Milk) 204
Spiral #1933 (Mint Green) 158
Thousand Eye #1000 134
Toy 135
Wakefield Fairy Lamps 194
Wakefield #1932 193

INDEX

Bibliography

Archer, Margaret and Douglas. *Imperial Glass*. Paducah, KY: Collector Books, 1978.

Barnett, Jerry. *Paden City, the Color Company*. Astoria, IL: Stevens Publishing Company, 1978.

Bickenheuser, Fred. *Tiffin Glassmasters*. Grove City, OH: Glassmasters Publication, 1979.

____. *Tiffin Glassmasters II*. Grove City, OH: Glassmasters Publication, 1981.

____. *Tiffin Glassmasters, III*. Grove City, OH: Glassmasters Publication, 1985.

Bones, Frances. *The Book of Duncan Glass*. Des Moines, IA: Wallace-Homestead Co., 1973.

Bredehoft, Neila and Tom. *Hobbs, Brock-unier & Co., Glass*. Paducah, KY: Collector Books, 1997.

____. *The Collector's Encyclopedia of Heisey Glass, 1925 – 1938*. Paducah, KY: Collector Books, 1993.

Breeze, George & Linda. *Mysteries of the Moon & Stars*. Paducah, KY: Image Graphics, Inc.

Burns, Mary Louise. *Heisey's Glassware of Distinction*. Mesa, AZ: Triangle Books, 1974.

Canton Glass Company, Inc. *Glassware by Canton*. Marion, IN: Canton Glass Company, 1954.

Conder, Lyle, Ed. *Collector's Guide to Heisey's Glassware for Your Table*. Glass City, IN: L.W. Book Sales, 1984.

Duncan & Miller Glass Co. *Hand-Made Duncan, Catalogue No. 89* (Reprint). Washington, PA: Duncan & Miller Co., copyright pending by Richard Harold and Robert Roach.

Duncan & Miller, Inc. *Hand-made Duncan, Catalogue No. 93*. Tiffin, OH: Duncan & Miller Division, U.S. Glass Company, Inc.

Felt, Tom & Bob O'Grady. *Heisey Candlesticks, Candelabra & Lamps*. Newark, OH: Heisey Collectors of American, Inc., 1984.

Felt, Tom and Elaine & Rich Stoer. *The Glass Candlestick Book, Vol. 1*. Paducah, KY: Collector Books, 2003

____. *Vol. 2*. Paducah, KY: Collector Books, 2003

____. *Vol. 3*. Paducah, KY: Collector Books, 2005

Florence, Gene & Cathy. *Elegant Glassware of the Depression Era, 12th Ed*. Paducah, KY: Collector Books, 2007.

____. *Collector's Encyclopedia of Depression Glass, 17th Ed*. Paducah, KY: Collector Books, 2006.

____. *Collectible Glassware of the 40s, 50s, and 60s, 8th Ed*. Paducah, KY: Collector Books, 2006.

____. *Anchor Hocking's Fire-King and More. 3rd Ed*. Paducah, KY: Collector Books, 2006.

Gallagher, Jerry. *A Handbook of Old Morgantown Glass, Vol. 1*. Minneapolis, MN: Merit Printing, 1995.

H.C. Fry Glass Society. *The Collectors' Encyclopedia of Fry Glassware*. Paducah, KY: Collector Books, 1990.

Heacock, William. *Opalescent Glass from A to Z*. Marietta, OH: Richardson Printing Corp. 1975.

Kerr, Ann. *Fostoria*. Paducah, KY: Collector Books, 1997 update.

____. *Fostoria, Vol. II*. Paducah, KY: Collector Books, 1997.

King, W.L. *Duncan & Miller Glass, Sec. Ed*. Venetia, PA: Victoria House Museum.

Krause, Gail. *The Encyclopedia of Duncan Glass*. Hicksville, NY: Exposition Press, 1976.

Measell, James. *New Martinsville Glass, 1900 – 1944*. Marietta, OH: Antique Publications, 1994.

____. *Fenton Glass, The 1980s Decade*. Marietta, OH: Glass Press, Inc. 1996.

____, editor. *Imperial Glass Encyclopedia, Vol. I*. National Imperial Glass Collectors' Society. Marietta, OH: The Glass Press, Inc., 1995.

____, editor. *Imperial Glass Encyclopedia, Vol. II*. Marietta, OH: The Glass Press, Inc., 1997.

Miller, Everett R. and Addie R. *The New Martinsville Glass Story Book II, 1920 – 1950*. Manchester, MI, Rymack Printing Company, 1975.

National Cambridge Collectors, Inc. *Genuine Handmade Cambridge, 1949 – 1953*. Paducah, KY: Collector Books, 1978.

____. *The Cambridge Glass Co., 1930 – 1934*. Paducah, KY: Collector Books, 1976.

____. *Colors in Cambridge Glass*. Paducah, KY: Collector Books, 1984.

Newark Heisey Collectors' Club. *Heisey by Imperial and Imperial Glass by Lenox*. Newark, OH: Heisey Collectors of America, Inc. 1980.

Newbound, Betty and Bill. *Collector's Encyclopedia of Milk Glass*. Paducah, KY: Collector Books, 1998.

Page, Bob and Dale Frederiksen. *A Collection of American Crystal*. Greensboro, NC: Page-Frederiksen Publishing Company, 1995.

____. *Tiffin is Forever*. Greensboro, NC: Page-Frederiksen Publishing Co., 1994.

Ream, Louise, Neila M., and Thomas H. Bredehoft. *Encyclopedia of Heisey Glassware, Vol. 1*. Newark, OH: Heisey Collectors of America, Inc., 1977.

Sferrazza, Julie. *Farber Brothers, Krome Kraft*. Marietta, OH: Antique Publications, 1988.

____. *Heisey on Parade*. Lombard, IL: Wallace-Homestead, 1985.

Viking Glass Company. *Treasured American Glass*. New Martinsville, WV: Viking Glass Company.

Vogel, Clarence W. *Heisey's First Ten Years...1896 – 1905*. Plymouth, OH: Heisey Publications, 1969.

____. *Heisey's Colonial Years...1906 – 1922*. Plymouth, OH: Heisey Publications, 1969.

____. *Heisey's Art and Colored Glass, 1922 – 1942*. Plymouth, OH: Heisey Publications, 1970.

____. *Heisey's Early and Late Years, 1896 – 1958*. Plymouth, OH: Heisey Publications, 1971.

Walker, Mary Lyle and Lynn. *The Cambridge Glass Co*. Newark, OH: Spencer Walker Press, 1974.

Weatherman, Hazel Marie. *Colored Glassware of the Depression Era, Book 2*. Springfield, MO: Weatherman Glassbooks, 1974.

____. *Fostoria, Its First Fifty Years*. Springfield, MO: The Weathermans, 1979.

____. *Price Trends to Colored Glassware of the Depression Era, Book 2*. Springfield, MO: Weatherman Glass Books, 1979.

Whitmyer, Margaret & Kenn. *Fenton Art Glass, 1907 – 1939*. Paducah, KY: Collector Books, 1996.

Wilson, Charles West. *Westmoreland Glass*. Paducah, KY: Collector Books, 1996.

Wilson, Jack D. *Phoenix and Consolidated Art Glass: 1926 – 1980*. Marietta, OH: Antique Publications, 1996.

BIBLIOGRAPHY

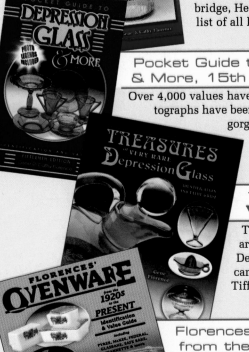

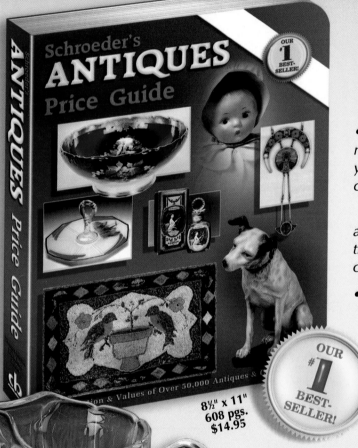